THE GRIEVING CHILD

A Parent's Guide

HELEN

FITZGERALD

A FIRESIDE BOOK
Published by
SIMON & SCHUSTER
New York ▼ London ▼ Toronto
Sydney ▼ Tokyo ▼ Singapore

FIRESIDE

Rockefeller Center
1230 Avenue of the Americas
New York, New York 10020

Copyright © 1992 by Helen Fitzgerald

FIRESIDE and colophon are registered trademarks
of Simon & Schuster Inc.

Designed by Diane Stevenson SNAP·HAUS GRAPHICS

Manufactured in the United States of America

10

Library of Congress Cataloging-in-Publication Data

Fitzgerald, Helen.
    The grieving child : a parents guide / Helen Fitzgerald.
        p. cm.
    "A Fireside book."
    Includes bibliographical references and index.
    1. Children and death. 2. Bereavement in children. 3. Grief in
children. 4. Child rearing. I. Title.
    B723.D3F58 1992   91-48211
    155.9'37'0240431—dc20   CIP

ISBN 0-671-76762-3

This book is dedicated to my second husband, Richard Olson, whose expert guidance and loving support gave me what I needed to write it, and to all the wonderful children who have come into my life bearing the burden of great losses, sadness, and distress. They have been my teachers, without whom this book could not have been written.

CONTENTS
▼▼▼▼▼▼▼▼▼

Contents

Contents

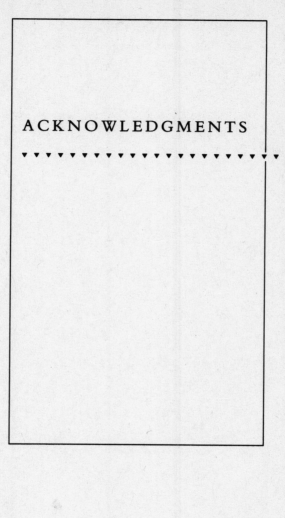

ACKNOWLEDGMENTS

Publication of this book provides me an opportunity to thank the many people who made it possible for me to become the director of a grief program, lecturer, death educator, and now, an author. In the difficult period before and after the death of my first husband I had wonderful support from doctors and colleagues at Fairfax Hospital in Falls Church, Virginia, where I worked as a creative therapist. One of these was Doris Herring, R.N., M.Ed., who served as a sounding board for my many frustrations. Another was Barbara (Cookie) Kerxton, B.A., my fellow creative therapist whose sense of humor helped preserve my sanity. And it was a social worker, Eileen Pearlman, who made me aware of a newly formed national support group for persons with life-threatening illness; it was called Make Today Count. She and I formed the third chapter of that organization. Later I began offering my services as a volunteer to work with cancer patients, thanks to the support and encouragement of Richard Binder, M.D., an oncologist. Bill Jacobs, an administrator at Fairfax, also gave me strong support, including the assistance of the hospital in providing me professional supervision by my teacher and mentor. Mila Tecala, LCSW, who was already becoming known for her work with dying patients.

Others who helped me get started were Peter Bloom, Ph.D., a psychologist who became my co-leader of Make Today Count; Lee Wick, M.A., then director of Prevention and Early Intervention at the Mount Vernon Center for Community Mental Health in Alexandria, Virginia, who hired me to direct the Center's grief program; Shirley Costello, Ph.D., director of the Center, who supported that decision and my program for eleven years before her retirement; Dan Leviton, Ph.D., professor of health education at the University of Maryland, who gave me my first lecture opportunity and who has encouraged me in my career ever since; Elisabeth Kübler-Ross, M.D., whose advice and counsel have been very important to me; numerous colleagues in the Association for Death Education and Counselling; and many other friends and associates whom I would mention but for the limitations of space.

I also want to thank my children—Patti Ann, Sarah, Chuck, and Mary—for exceptional patience and understanding during those tough early years as I was developing my career.

Finally, I want to acknowledge the contributions of my literary agent, Anne Edelstein, and my editors, Tony Sciarra and Sheridan Hay, who held my hand and guided me though the completion of this book.

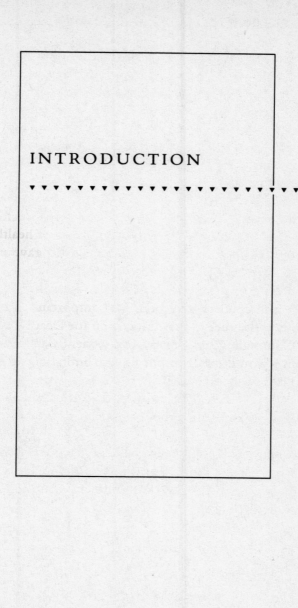

INTRODUCTION

▼▼▼▼▼▼▼▼▼▼▼▼▼▼▼▼▼▼▼▼▼▼▼▼▼▼▼▼▼▼▼▼▼▼▼▼▼

Every year hundreds of thousands of children in the United States and millions throughout the world experience the death of a parent, grandparent, or other close relative, shattering their seemingly secure worlds. All too often their surviving parents, preoccupied with their own grief but thinking they are doing the right thing, hide their true feelings, tell their children little or nothing about what has happened, leave them out of all serious family discussions, send them away at the time of the funeral, and somehow manage to ignore their children's need to grieve the losses that have so drastically altered their lives.

There is nothing evil about the way these adults neglect the emotional needs of their children; it is just that they don't know, or have never given thought to, the emotional impact that the death of a parent or other close relative can have on a child. If they knew, they would not allow a child's fantasies to cloud reality, or a child's anger to lead to destructive acts. If they knew, they would not allow a child's unresolved grief to continue into adulthood, imposing a burden of anguish for as long as a lifetime.

Even though many adults now understand something about the process of grief, this way of dealing with children's grief is still altogether too common. And the only way to alter this pattern is for people to become aware of the tremendous importance of being truthful, open, and caring, the importance of allowing children to ask questions and confirm the reality confronting them, the importance of allowing them to go through the painful but therapeutic process of grief.

Some years ago Helen Fitzgerald, whom I met when her first husband was dying of cancer, began a pioneering experiment in her role as Director of the Grief Program at the Mt. Vernon Center for Community Mental Health in Alexandria, Virginia. Designed for young children who have suffered great, often traumatic, losses such as suicide deaths and murders, her experiment combined death education with the idea of a support group, previously considered inappropriate for young children. Its success, attested to by the teachers and parents of these troubled children, has broken new ground in the mental health field.

In the course of this work Ms. Fitzgerald became aware of the need for a parent's guide which could be a kind of primer for parents in helping their children through the process of grief. This book was written to fill that need. It begins with cases of adults who have carried unresolved grief from their childhood and goes on to address in detail the many things parents can do to help children with their grief, thus avoiding such a fate.

I commend *The Grieving Child* to every parent, either to help a child grieving the death of a loved one, or to help prepare the parent and child for losses that are yet to come. Mortal as we all are, they will come.

Elisabeth Kübler-Ross, M.D.
Headwaters, Virgina
March, 1990

A VERY
PERSONAL
STATEMENT

What I share with you in this book comes not so much from books or academic pursuits as from life—what I have learned as the wife of a cancer patient, a widow, the mother of four fatherless children, and, finally, as a therapist trying to help grieving people.

I am a person whose career began with tragedy: the long illness and death of my first husband. One day as I sat with my husband, who lay in a coma in the hospital, a medical resident noticed me reading a book about death and dying. Knowing that my husband's illness had gone on for years, the young doctor asked me if I would be willing to share my experiences with a group of doctors and social workers. Surprised and flattered, I consented, but then wondered if I were losing my mind. I had never talked in front of an audience before and had never shared with strangers anything as personal as this. In spite of these misgivings, I managed to get through that first talk, and from it came the realization that I had something to say: something that could be of help to others in similar situations. I didn't know it at the time, but it was at this moment that my career began.

When my husband died after nearly three years of terminal illness, our children had reached the ages of eight to fifteen. Patti was fifteen; Sarah, thirteen; Chuck, twelve; and Mary, eight. Looking back, I shudder at some of the mistakes I made with them. I readily understand—now— why they were angry with me when I belatedly told them that their father was dying. Like so many parents, I had assumed that I should protect them from sad or disturbing news. I was wrong.

The first sign that my husband might have a problem had appeared twelve years earlier when I opened a medical bill one day and discovered that he'd had an electroencephalogram. When I asked him about this, he refused to discuss it other than to say it was "nothing." From time to time after that I noticed him having a seizure or spell of some sort, but these episodes were brief and didn't seem so bad. He would clear his throat, rub his head, and sometimes stop talking in the middle of a sentence. Sometimes he would get very pale as if he were going to faint. Then he would resume whatever he was doing.

Years passed with nothing said about these abnormalities. My husband was unwilling to discuss them, and I in turn said nothing to the children, partly because he refused to acknowledge that the things occurred, and partly because I didn't know what to make of them myself. Then during the summer of 1971, when we were at a lake cottage with relatives, the seizures became noticeably more severe, lasting not just a few minutes but an hour or more. That fall he finally was diagnosed with a brain tumor, possibly benign because of its slow growth. Still, we said very little to the children, even when my husband had brain surgery to remove what proved to be a large malignant tumor.

Perhaps it was an attitude of the past that has changed—I hope so—but the doctor discouraged me from telling my husband that he had cancer. Of course, this meant not telling the children, either, for they could not be expected to keep such a secret. When he came home after six weeks in the hospital the children saw a very different father, changed in appearance and, sadly, in personality. He now had to wear his left arm in a sling. His left leg required a brace, and he had to use a cane to walk. Worse still, he had become highly irritable, often lashing out at me and the children. Although he went back to work part time for a period, he saw his role as husband, father, and breadwinner waning, and this contributed to his anger and frustration. When it became obvious that he couldn't work any longer and was forced to retire, life at home turned even worse. Yet through all this the children were told little or nothing. Although I knew that he had cancer, and he must have known, that word never passed our lips. The children were kept in the dark. For all they knew, their father might still recover and be his old self again. This is the way most people dealt with life-threatening illness at the time.

I know now that our children sensed that more was going on than they were being told. They were often irritable, exhibiting anger and making what seemed to me impossible demands. When, shortly after my husband was admitted to the hospital for the last time, I finally told them that he was dying, there was almost a sense of relief. They told me that they had known that something was wrong, but, since they didn't know what, they hadn't known what they could do to help. After that we began to pull together, and a sense of closeness replaced the tension in our household.

Two months later my husband went into a coma, which lasted seven months before he died. It was during this period that I was asked to give that talk. As a reward I was invited to an informal lunch with Dr. Elisabeth Kübler-Ross, author of the book I had been reading. During the lunch of deli sandwiches eaten on boxes behind the stage where she was about to speak, I had many questions to ask her. I wanted to know what to do with my children and how I could help them through this terrible time. Her response was the beginning of my awareness of the importance of openness and honesty in dealing with one's children. She told me that children need to be informed of important things that are happening to their loved ones. And she urged that I give my children an opportunity to visit their dying and comatose father—that night, if possible. Later, in speaking to the luncheon group, she said she had just met someone who wanted to use her experience as the wife of a dying husband to help others in similar circumstances.

As it turned out, only Mary chose to visit her father, but since it was Christmas time, all of the children helped decorate a small Christmas tree to convey their love. Sometime later Sarah also visited him. It was the last time any of them saw their father alive. He died about three months later.

Inspired by Dr. Kübler-Ross, I volunteered to work with terminally ill patients at the hospital where I then was employed. An oncologist there knew me from having attended my husband the previous year, and he agreed to allow me to visit some of his patients. About the same time I organized the third chapter in the nation of the self-help group, Make Today Count, formed to help people with life-threatening diseases like cancer. I have continued to work with that group through the years.

In 1977 there was an opening for someone to conduct a grief program for the large county in which I live; it was to be the first such program in a community mental health center anywhere in the nation. Someone with a doctorate, or at least a master's degree, was sought, but because of the volunteer work I had been doing, combined with several years' work as a creative therapist in a psychiatric unit, specialized training from professionals, self study, and my personal experience with tragedy, the center's director decided to take a chance on me. I am still there, operating a program that includes individual counseling, seminars for the widowed, lecturing, writing, and leading self-help groups of many kinds.

During my early years in this work I became aware of the need to help grieving children, yet it was assumed that children lack the maturity to help each other in group situations. I then developed what I call an educational/support model. It consists of using educational tools to teach children about the grieving process, then allowing them to interact with one another in a group setting. It has been very successful and has brought me requests for information and advice from professionals throughout the world. It forms the heart of this book.

Looking back on my life since that awful day my husband died, I feel that in death he gave me a gift he could never have anticipated: a life work to complete. While one never forgets a lost loved one, I have discovered that the life of a survivor can be rich, rewarding, and happy. I wish the same for you.

BEFORE
YOU BEGIN
THIS BOOK

This is not a book you have to read from beginning to end. If you like, you can simply look up topics that concern you. These might include how to deal with your grieving child's anger, guilt, or depression. I mention this because you yourself may be dealing with the enormousness of grief, struggling with changed circumstances following the death of a loved one, and worrying about what is happening to your child. For a while you may not be able to concentrate on a whole book from start to finish. If that describes your situation, use this book as a handbook, referring to it as questions arise. A paragraph numbering system is intended to help you with cross references. All subjects are listed in the table of contents and index. I hope that you will, in time, read it all the way through, as I have included in it many ideas for helping you and your child.

Of course, this book is not just for people in grief; it is a book of advice for all parents whose children may face one day the terrible loss of someone central to their lives, from a father, mother, or adored grandparent to a close friend or playmate or even a beloved pet. And what child doesn't face that possibility?

The death of a loved one can shatter a child's secure world, yet out of such a family crisis can come a bond between parent and child that will sustain a closeness between them for the rest of their lives. This book is intended to help you and your child along that path.

While there are various approaches taken by mental health professionals to the problems of their clients, my approach has no scientific name. If it had a name, it would have to be something like "Direct" or "Clear." At the same time, it is always gentle and loving, never aggressive or demanding. Listening carefully to what my young clients say, I find that they not only are capable of hearing words like "killed," "dead," and "forever," but they begin to feel better when they can talk openly about the dark things that are troubling them.

Chapter 1 talks about beginnings and endings: What can you do now, regardless of your personal situation, to acquaint your child with the way life ends? How can you answer your child's questions in a way that he or she can understand?

Children react differently to death than do adults. These differences depend on their ages, the circumstances of a death, and their relationship to the deceased. Chapter 2 discusses these differences.

Chapter 3 spells out ways to prepare your child for the possible death of someone close. It will help you think about and discuss funerals in general, special funerals for children to attend, burial of the dead, and cemetery visits.

Chapter 4 goes into specifics about the emotional responses children may have, such as denial, anger, guilt, and depression, and ways to deal with them. The many suggestions here stem from my work with children's bereavement groups on using drawing, puppets, games, balloons, and the like. Use these suggestions if you have a child who is wrestling with such emotions.

Chapter 5 deals with adjusting to a new life, from the immediate issue of going back to school to larger ongoing role changes. How will your family handle holidays? What about the child's unfinished business with the deceased? Later, how will he or she adjust to the dating and remarriage of a widowed parent?

Chapter 6 provides help for those parents who discover after the fact that they could have been more helpful to their children at the time of a death. It is never too late to resolve these issues.

Chapter 7 brings the discussion full circle by addressing those parents and other adults who may still be carrying the effects of unresolved childhood grief themselves.

Finally, don't be afraid of reading about death. The more you know about what to expect, the better able you are to deal with it and to help your child accept that part of life we most want to put out of our minds but is common to us all: its ending.

chapter **1**

▼▼

INTRODUCING YOUR CHILD TO THE REALITY OF DEATH

Our lives consist of beginnings and endings, most of which we share with our children: the beginning of an ice cream cone to the last savored licks, the beginning of an exciting trip until the sleepy arrival at some distant destination, sunrise followed by sunset, the invocation followed by the benediction. Since death is the natural ending of life, this too must be shared with our children if they are going to have a chance to mature normally and see the world for what it is. Unpleasant as it is to think about, hard as it is to apply to those we love, much as we would like to believe otherwise, all of us are mortal.

THINGS ANY PARENT CAN DO NOW
▼▼▼▼▼▼▼▼▼▼▼▼▼▼▼▼▼▼▼▼▼▼▼▼▼▼▼▼▼▼▼▼▼▼▼

Most of this book deals with helping your child grieve the death of a loved one. But you don't have to wait until a personal tragedy occurs to begin educating your son or daughter about the mortality that we all share. If you have the luxury of preparing your child in advance for the reality of death, so much the better. You can help your child understand what death actually is, whether someone has just died or whether such an event is at this time only a distant but painful possibility.

1. Take stock of your own "death history" and your own feelings about death. Before you begin talking to your child about the death of a loved one or about death in general, be sure *you* know where you stand. What are your private feelings about this highly charged subject? You don't want your child's view of death to be shaped by any lingering inhibitions that you might have. The more you understand yourself, the easier it will be to avoid letting those feelings influence your child.

Ask yourself the following questions:

- What was your first experience with death?
- How did you learn about the death?
- How did you feel about what happened?
- Were you "protected" from the reality of what had happened?
- Were you prepared for what you would see when you went to the funeral home?
- Were you discouraged from crying or otherwise showing your emotions?
- Were you comforted or left to fend for yourself?
- Were you made to do things you were not prepared for, such as kissing the body?
- How did your family's religious beliefs influence your thinking about death? Do you hold the same beliefs today?
- What were your childhood superstitions at the time?

When I was a child I was told that whenever you heard an owl hoot, someone would die. I spent whole summers sleeping with a feather tick over my head to keep from hearing an owl hoot and causing someone to die. I also remember my first death experience, at the age of nine, when our family's pet dog, whom I loved very much and regarded as my own, was struck and killed by a car on the road next to my parents' farm. I learned of it when I was awakened by footsteps on the driveway. When I looked out, I saw my mother carrying Jocky's dead body. How terrible I felt, and how angry I was at the hit-and-run driver who had killed our dog! Getting dressed quickly, I walked out into the pasture to be by myself, to cry and to think about Jocky and what life was going to be like without that sweet, affectionate little dog. Oh, how I missed her! To this day I have never loved a pet as much as I loved Jocky. After a while, I started walking home. I met my mother, who was coming out to console me. Together we walked back to the house. There she took out her jewelry box, which she knew I treasured, and let me pick out something for myself. It was a very loving gesture, making me feel that she understood my pain.

What I did next may tell us something about the inherent capacity of children to respond appropriately to their feelings: To cope with my anger I wrote a letter to the anonymous driver of that car telling him (I assumed it was a man) what a terrible thing he had done, and then I buried the letter with Jocky's body.

Recalling your first death experience could help you prepare to talk to your child about this painful subject. What is your feeling about showing your emotions when a loved one dies? The more you understand yourself and your own "death history," the better able you will be to help your child deal with the reality of death. (If you are uncomfortable with your own "death history," you may find it helpful to turn to Chapter 7, "Resolving Childhood Grief as an Adult.")

2. Use the correct language. When talking to your child about someone who has died, say the word. Don't use euphemisms like "we have lost him" or "he is walking in the valley of shadows," because they can lead to misinterpretation. Try to imagine how your child could interpret those phrases. Other euphemisms clearly are designed to confuse, such as "he is sleeping." (For an example of such confusion, see "Grandma, Why Are You So Cold?" in Chapter 7.) Practice in front of a mirror, if necessary, so you will be prepared to speak to your son or daughter using the real words that apply to the situation—words like "dead," "killed," "cancer," "stroke," "heart attack," "strangled," or "murdered." This may be hard for you if you were brought up in an environment that was different from the one you are striving to create for your child or if you were "protected" from the reality of unhappy events by evasions. But try it.

You may want to ask your child if she is hearing any words she doesn't understand. I recall asking this of a little girl whose father had died, and she replied, "Yes." The word she didn't know the meaning of was "widow." Your child may be puzzled by other words like this, and you can help her immensely by telling her what they mean.

3. Have a book on death in your child's library. Let your son or daughter perceive that you see death as a natural and accepted part of life. I find that books can play an important part in opening up this difficult subject with children. First, reading to a child is a natural, comfortable, and enriching activity for both parent and child. The warmth that occurs here can generate a lasting closeness between you and your child. Books are often helpful when it comes time to talk about something that is difficult. It is easier to address a painful topic when you have already created this caring atmosphere and when you already have read the words of authors who have dealt with it in an honest way, and who are not emotionally involved in your personal loss.

There are many excellent books to choose from. *Charlotte's Web* by E. B. White is a wonderful book to read to a child of elementary school age to introduce the topic of death. An animated version of this book is now available on home video as well. Another book for the same age range is *Aarvy Ardvaark Finds Hope* by Donna O'Toole. This is a delightful book to read to a child, especially if you stop often to translate the animal story into human terms and then into your own situation. A bibliography of recommended children's books dealing with death appears at the end of the book.

4. Some cautions on looking for a book on death. Examine the book carefully before purchasing it. Listen to the words and try to translate them as your child would, as in the examples below. Ask yourself: Is this an honest book, conveying the information you would like your child to have, or does it somehow deny the reality of death? For example, implying that the dead can be brought back to life conveys a dishonest message. Is it needlessly frightening? For example, a death figure stalking bad children, is likely to create fear. Does it give wrong information? The implication that only old people die, for example, may confuse children.

One book I came across portrayed death as an old man with a book of names; when your name came up, it was your turn to die. You can guess how a child, exposed to such an idea, might react in church or synagogue when the pastor or rabbi walks in, looking rather old and intimidating in his flowing robes, carrying a large book. A book that teaches children that they can outsmart death, too, can only breed trouble. Make sure you aren't creating that kind of problem for your child.

5. Look for death education opportunities. If your situation allows it, be on the alert for opportunities in which your child can be taught about death, but without the emotional impact that the death of a loved one will have. This might be as simple as finding a dead plant or a dead bird. In the case of a dead bird you might gently nudge the bird to show that the bird does not respond. Point out how limp the body is.

A good way to explain death to your child is to speak of it as the absence of life. Talk about what life meant to this bird: that it could fly, that it could see, that it could sing, that it could eat, that it could "go to the bathroom," but that now that the bird is dead, it cannot and never again will be able to do any of those things.

Then talk about feelings. Seeing the body of the dead bird, knowing this bird will never be the same again, can make a person sad. It's okay to feel sad and to cry. Then decide with your child what to do with the body of the dead bird. Discuss options. You could just leave the body there to decay naturally, or you could wrap it up and put it into the trash, or you could wrap it up and bury it someplace. Most children will vote for the burial. Children love ritual and ceremony. They may want to have a real funeral with flowers, songs, and a headstone. No matter what the decision is, this can be a learning experience for your child, a time to learn that death is real, final, and natural, and most importantly, a time to say goodbye.

Some years ago we had an unusual experience at my house. My twelve-year-old daughter called me at work to say that our very old black cat, Little, seemed to be dying. I asked what gave her that idea, and she said the cat kept meowing all the time and looked sick. I drove home and discovered my daughter and a friend, our dog, and our white cat maintaining a death watch over Little, who was lying in a basket in the kitchen, wrapped in a sheet, meowing weakly. We then talked about Little: how we had acquired her many years ago, what good times we had had with her, and what happens when the body dies. The children had all sorts of questions. For example, my daughter asked me if I had ever seen a person die, and I said yes, I had. I suppose the most interesting part of this for the children was that the two other pets seemed to know what was happening and lay quietly providing company to their dying friend. After a while I told the children I thought that Little was in no great pain, but I gave them the choice of taking the cat to the veterinarian's to be given an injection or of allowing her to die naturally. They chose the latter. As the vigil continued, I gave them permission to go about their affairs while I worked in the kitchen, keeping an eye on the three pets. After a few hours Little did die, and the children elected to have the cat buried in our yard, where her remains now lie beneath a lovely Chinese elm (see Topic 21). Although my daughter, whose own father had by then died, already knew a lot about death, this was nevertheless an occasion to ask questions she hadn't asked before and to become more comfortable with this somber side of reality.

6. Far from an experience to be endured alone, the death of a loved one is an opportunity for bonding. Our children are always included in life's beginnings: what joy there is when a baby is born, and how eager we are to share such news with them! But the same is frequently not true when life ends, when someone we love dies. We may be so uncomfortable with this unpleasant reality that we exclude our children from most or all of the events associated with a death and provide them with little or no information about what is happening. In the mistaken belief that we are protecting our children, we deprive ourselves and our children of one of life's great opportunities for bonding: the sharing of a deeply felt, painful, and sad experience.

While life provides many opportunities for bonding with one's child, those of us who can be honest with our children and can talk openly about a personal loss of great magnitude have a special opportunity to develop a trust that may help carry us through many future ups and downs that threaten the parent–child relationship—drugs, for example, or the child's experimentation with sex.

In the first days after a loved one has died, you might

set aside a certain time of day when you and your child can talk. While the death of your loved one will certainly be the thing you talk most about initially, after a while you should find this regular "talk time" an occasion to discuss all sorts of things that are going on in your child's life. It can be an enriching experience for both of you.

chapter **2**

▼▼▼▼▼▼▼▼▼▼▼▼▼▼▼▼▼▼▼▼▼▼▼▼▼▼▼▼▼▼▼▼▼

HOW CHILDREN REACT TO DEATH

Do children really grieve? Parents often ask this question as they wrestle with the question of whether or not to include their child in the rituals surrounding a death. I believe they ask it also because, even though there are some similarities, childhood grief *is* different from the grief experienced by adults. Adults have a clearer idea of the finality of death. When a spouse dies, the remaining spouse is reminded of this every minute of the day. Getting up in the morning, choosing the clothes one wears and the food one serves, performing chores once shared, and deciding how one spends one's evening time, and especially night time, are constant reminders that someone is missing. Adults feel grief more intensely and more compactly. Children, by comparison, haven't had many of the experiences life has to offer, nor are they cognitively able to understand death as we do. Thus they grieve without the same level of comprehension of what is happening to them, for they have not had the experience of the finality that accompanies someone's death.

  7. Children grieve more sporadically than adults. Children who are grieving the death of a parent will experience that grief over many years, but without the intensity of their early grief. They will be in touch with their grief especially when big events occur in their lives, such as gaining the honor roll, earning a merit badge, winning a swimming competition, going to camp, having a first date. This process will continue even as they advance into adulthood, reminding them of what they have lost as they approach graduation from high school and college, marriage, the birth of babies, new promotions—all moments they would have wanted to share with that person who died when they were young.

8. Children are more capable than adults of putting grief aside. Because the emotion of grief is so hard for them to handle, children often will focus for a time on more pleasant things. When a thirteen-year-old girl was told that her father had died, she responded with, "Can we get a kitten?" She later told me that she had wanted to think of something "fun," something that would divert her from the pain she was feeling. While working with children in a neighborhood in which a young girl had been murdered, I observed a seven-year-old girl draw pictures depicting her recent birthday—here again an attempt to focus on something pleasant. This is not atypical of children confronting such harsh reality.

9. Children don't have to deal with the many reminders of loss in the same way as do adults. Children are spared dealing with the tedious details that death brings: the funeral arrangements, the will, the bank accounts, the legal work, the insurance policies, and all of the practical matters that come flooding in on the surviving adults after the death of a loved one. In not having to attend to such matters, however, children miss some of the reality of death. This creates the need for them to deal with that reality at their *own* level, and parents must help them do so.

10. As they grow up, children go through tremendous developmental changes. With each stage of development the child perceives death differently.

A preschool child cannot comprehend the word "forever." You can tell a toddler that Daddy has died and that when someone dies, he is gone forever. The child will go out to play and in an hour come back to ask the mother, "When is Daddy coming home?" To this child, one hour is "forever." This belief is further supported by some of the television cartoons children watch. Take the classic cartoon situation in which an animal character is smashed or thrown off a cliff, in effect killed, only to bounce back to life in the next frame, looking no worse for the experience. Thus children may be led to believe that death is reversible. You can help your child by avoiding programs of this kind and by making clear to him or her the difference between television and real life.

Be consistent with your answers to questions about the reality of death. Your child needs to hear the same information over and over until it begins to sink in. "Daddy has died and when you die, you can never come back. He is gone forever."

Young school-age children are beginning to learn that death is real. Perhaps their teacher has read to them a book about death. However, as long as death is still outside their circle of family and friends, they are likely to be caught up in magical thinking and to feel that if you are careful and smart enough, you can avoid death. Children this age can feel very powerful. If a death does occur, they may feel guilty, being convinced that if they had been at the scene and had acted in time, they could have prevented the death from happening. Ordinarily children of this age believe that death happens only to old people, and because of this belief, you may find a child asking you if you are old yet. If a distant or aging relative should die, this could be an opportunity to expose the child to a funeral and to the finality that comes with death.

Older school-age children tend to see death in the form of some tangible being, such as a ghost, bogeyman, or a hooded figure with scythe. This is the age of telling ghost stories and of imagined adventures in the cemetery alone at night, where a hand may reach up out of the grave and grab a person. Children of this age know that death can happen to young as well as old people and they know death has many different causes. However, they still think that death usually happens to other people. At about the age of ten, the child begins to have real fears that a parent might die, and may have nightmares about this. By this time, the child may have experienced the death of a loved pet. This is an opportunity to continue teaching the child about death. Do not immediately replace the pet with a new one in the hope that your child will be less affected by the loss. Allow the child to be involved with decisions surrounding the pet's death. Discuss options of disposing of the body: of wrapping the body up and placing it in the trash, of letting the veterinarian dispose of the body, or of having a burial with rituals (see Topic 21).

Teenagers are fascinated with death and often spend time fantasizing about their own deaths, often to the dismay of their parents. They wonder who would come to their funerals, how badly everyone would feel, and what rituals would be included in the ceremonies. Even at this advanced age, however, teens still are not really in touch with the finality of death or the impossibility of their really enjoying their own funerals. Death is romanticized in many of the books they read, such as *Romeo and Juliet.* They may even find themselves challenging death by fast driving, experimenting with drugs, taking unnecessary risks, or engaging in other potentially dangerous activities.

EXPLAINING DEATH
▼▼▼▼▼▼▼▼▼▼▼▼▼▼▼▼▼▼▼▼

11. What is "dead?" This is one of the most difficult questions to answer and one of the questions parents most dread. How do you explain death? I like to turn this question around and ask the child, "What is life?" Recently I was working with a group of children and their parents who were concerned about the murder of a young neighborhood girl. I started to explain death in this way: "I am alive," I said. "I can breathe." With this idea in mind, we went around the room. Each person there, parents included, picked up on the theme. "I am alive. I can see."

"I am alive. I can dance." "I am alive. I can listen to music." And so on. After everyone had spoken, I said, "When that is all gone, that's what dead is." Suddenly there was a hush throughout the room as the children and their parents grasped the significance of that word. So explaining what "life" is, as we know it in this world, helps us to explain to children what "dead" is (see Topics 3 and 5).

12. Religion can play a part in explaining death. Death provides an opportunity to teach your child the religious beliefs you want him or her to live by. If you believe that there is life after death, this can be a source of great solace for your child. But there are certain common "religious" explanations you would do well to avoid. For example: "God loved your father so much that He has taken him to heaven." A boy may interpret that to mean that God took his dad away because he didn't love him enough. A girl may feel that since she didn't love her dad enough, she is being punished.

Another phrase to be careful of is: "It's all part of God's plan." What plan? Is it part of God's plan to have a mother killed by a plane dropping on top of her car (this actually happened)? Most parents want to teach children that God is a loving God, not a God that allows airplanes to fall on cars. Many children (and adults) find themselves angry with God for allowing a death to happen. They feel frustrated and question their faith. I remember a father who was dying of cancer. He had three daughters and a wife who frequently told me confidently, "My husband will get well; we are praying to God every day and God answers prayers." The husband called me into his hospital room one day and made a statement I will never forget.

He said, "You must help me talk to my family. I know that God answers prayers, but He doesn't always answer them the way we ask Him to. He may answer my prayers by sending me to heaven." Unfortunately, there are no easy answers to questions of this kind, and you should not hesitate to ask for the help of your own pastor or rabbi when you feel you need help.

Sometimes, heaven is described as such a wonderful place that you may hear your daughter (or son) wishing she could die and also go there. This is a fairly common reaction and should not cause undue alarm. If you hear this from your child, you should emphasize three things: how much you miss Dad, too; how much you love her; and how much you need her here with you. However, if she continues talking in this vein, you might consult with a professional for advice (see Topic 63 and "When to Be Concerned" under Topic 64).

Recently, in one of my children's groups, the children made paper bag puppets. One puppet was to represent the child and the second was to represent the parent who had died. The puppets gave the children an opportunity to have a "pretend" conversation with the deceased parent. Over and over I heard the child puppet asking the parent puppet, "What is it like up there?" "Is there a Disney World up there?" "Is the food as good as Mom says it is?" "Do you have ice cream every day?" "Is it true you don't hurt even if you fall down?" And "Is it true that you don't have homework up there?" You might use this technique with your own child, giving him or her the opportunity to ask some of those otherwise unstated questions, and giving you the opportunity to suggest realistic answers.

DIFFERENT DEATH SITUATIONS
▼ ▼

13. When death strikes without warning. It's one thing when the person who has died is elderly or when there has been a long illness, such as cancer, and the child has been involved with the grieving process before the death occurred. In this situation the child would have seen the natural progression of aging or the natural deterioration of the person suffering a long-term illness. Some grief work would have been completed before the death occurred, and perhaps there would have been a sense of relief when the death did occur (see Topic 30). A seven-year-old girl whose father was dying of a malignant brain tumor said at the time of the Christmas holiday, "Wouldn't it be nice if Daddy died on Christmas, the day Jesus was born?" Because this child had been included in the dying process, she had completed much of her grief work and was now ready to let her father die.

It's another thing, however, when the death has occurred more or less without warning, such as by heart attack or car accident. In such cases there has been no opportunity to see the physical changes in a dying person which would help the child come to terms with the approach of death. The entire family may be sent reeling from the blow and may have little time to think about the special needs of a child. Sometimes a child will be left to fend for himself (or herself) until and unless an adult in the family realizes he needs help—realizes that because he is a child, because he lacks an adult's perspective, because he is so vulnerable, his needs are at least as great, if not greater, than those of the adults around him.

A surviving parent, grandparent or other relative needs to take the child aside and tell him precisely what has happened, to answer his questions, to encourage an expression of his feelings, to explain to him what it means to die, to give him an opportunity to say goodbye in his own way to the person who has died, to include him in planning for the funeral and in the funeral itself, and to offer the love and support that he so desperately needs in order to resolve his grief over the loss that he, too, has suffered (see Topics 32, 34, and 38).

14. How do you explain suicide to a child? This is a tough one. Your child needs to be told about the death as soon as possible. She needs to be told everything you fear she will hear from relatives, friends and their parents. She needs to have this information come from *you.* (See Topic 32.) Again, this is an opportunity to bond with your child and to underscore your intention always to be just as honest as possible with her. (See Topic 6.)

Start by putting your child in a position where you are touching each other, perhaps on your lap. Children need lots of touching to feel secure. (See "Touch Therapy" in Topic 66.) Then tell her you have something very sad to tell her and that sometimes when one feels sad one cries, and that crying is okay. You might add that talking about this sad thing can cause you to cry, and that when you cry you need hugs. This will give her something to do when you cry and she will feel less frightened. Now you must go on to say, "Daddy died today." Usually the child will ask questions. Answer them as they come and as simply as possible. Don't give too much detail. Then comes the question, "How did Daddy die?" Your response may be something like this: "Sometimes we can't understand why people die in the way they do. When someone dies of cancer, heart attack, or an auto accident, we can understand it more. But sometimes people die in a different way. They do it to themselves. Do you know what that's called?" (Children will hear the word "suicide" from others; it is better if it comes from you first.) You might continue, "Sometimes people have an illness of the mind that causes them to kill themselves. They have it; *you* don't, *I* don't. It's hard to understand, and it *has nothing to do* with me or you. I didn't and you didn't do anything to cause this." Invite your child to come talk to you if she starts feeling bad or responsible for the death.

The next dreaded question may be, "How did he do it?" Again your child needs to know, but spare the graphic details. You might say, "This is hard for me to tell you, but I will. He had a gun and he shot himself." Or "He took a rope and hanged himself." Or "He went into the car and closed all the windows and kept the car running and the poison gas killed him." If your child asks, "What did he look like?" you can start with something like, "What do you think he looked like?" This may give you some insight into your child's imaginings about this tragic event. Some children will demand to know more of the details. These can be given in simple form without going into great depth (see Topic 32). If too much is kept hidden, however, I worry about what your child will imagine. Sometimes their imaginings can be worse than the truth. Again, I want to emphasize the importance of inviting your child to come to you if she has questions or hears disturbing comments that require factual answers.

15. Children find a suicide death confusing. One little girl wrote a "pretend" letter to her father who had killed himself, saying, "You said you loved me, but how could you do this to me?" The mother of this child explained that her father did love her but that because of the illness he had had in his mind, he could not think clearly and his thoughts were jumbled. She also reassured her daughter that her father knew she loved him.

Because suicide is such a difficult subject to discuss with a child, don't hesitate to ask for professional help if you find the going more than you can handle.

16. Murder is another difficult death to explain. As in suicide your child needs to be told as soon as you are able. The facts must be given in as simple a form as possible (see Topic 32). Let him know that he may be hearing all sorts of rumors and that they should be shared with you so the two of you can find out the truth. Many rumors create added frustration and fears for everyone.

In working with a neighborhood in which a ten-year-old girl had been assaulted and then murdered, I found that the primary concern of the children was the fear that something similar would happen to them. I found it necessary to spend time talking to them about things that they could do to feel safe, such as making sure their mothers or fathers knew where they are at all times; always going outdoors with a friend or two, never by oneself; never straying far from home; knowing where to run for help; and making a lot of noise to draw attention if threatened by an assailant. I also said that if they were not comfortable with an adult, it would be okay to walk away or not answer when spoken to.

Then I asked the children if they had been hearing any words they didn't know the meaning of. Out of this came, "Yeah, what is asphyxiation?" Abduction was another. In answering such questions, one either can explain the words or get the dictionary and look them up. We then discussed what a funeral is, and why we have funerals. We talked about how funerals help us face the reality that someone is really dead, and talked about the opportunity they give us to say goodbye and to let the family know we share some of their sorrow (see Topics 35 and 38).

It is hard for children to understand that another human being can kill someone. They are still at the age of dependency on adults for food, shelter, clothing, and emotional needs. When you try to explain to them that there are people who are bad out there, people who are capable of harming you, it can be so threatening that the child may retreat into fantasy. When the ten-year-old was murdered, one child said, "She was kidnapped, killed, and then a big bug bit her and she died." The reality was more than this child could understand and he wanted to translate the death into something less frightening. I gently explained that, while most grown-ups love children and want to protect them, once in a while there may be a bad person who would do what this person did.

In a death as violent as murder, do not be alarmed if you see your daughter acting out the murder as she perceives it may have been. This is a way of getting feelings out. Take this opportunity to talk to her, asking questions about the death and the play-acting you have just seen. If, however, she seems to be obsessing about the murder and you feel that her displays are more than you expected to see coming from your daughter, consult a professional who has had experience working with children in death situations.

RELATIONSHIPS TO THE DECEASED

▼▼▼▼▼▼▼▼▼▼▼▼▼▼▼▼▼▼▼▼▼▼▼

17. Death of a parent. If your spouse has died, you may notice your child seemingly not grieving (see Topics 7–9). Much of his life may continue to be normal, and as long as one parent remains, there is someone to provide for many of his needs, emotional and otherwise. However, we are learning that children who have a parent die often fantasize about their own deaths, seeing death as a way to regain the company of the deceased. If heaven is such a wonderful place, why not go there? The surviving parent, having to deal with his or her own grief, is probably not too easy to be with just now, so why not join the deceased parent?

It may come as a shock when the surviving parent hears the child scream out, "I want to die so I can be with my Dad (or Mom)." If this happens to you, keep in mind that your child does not really mean he wants to leave you forever. The fact is that he is not really in touch with the finality of those words. Take it as an opportunity to discuss this death wish with your son, but don't be panicked by it. (It's quite possible that you may have been feeling much the same way, fantasizing about going to sleep and never waking up.) Let him know that you understand how he feels but stress how important he is to you, and, most importantly, how much you love him. Children need that reassurance, particularly at times like this. If such reassurance doesn't seem to be working, consider discussing this with a professional.

We have learned that children who have a parent die frequently face difficulties developing personal relationships in later life. There is an underlying fear of being abandoned as they were when the parent died. To avoid this, we must be aware that children do grieve, even if that grief is not readily apparent, and we must help them express their grief.

18. Death of a grandparent. When an aged grandparent dies, you may notice very little displayed grief. To children this is natural. You grow up and you grow old, you have a good life, and then you die. However, the closer the child is to the grandparent, or the more involved she or he is with the grandparent, the more grief you will see.

It is in this time that you may notice your child asking you if you are old yet. For the parent of a young child the usual answer is no; in any case, the child needs reassurance that you expect to live a long time.

Because it is common today for children and grandparents to live long distances apart and to see each other infrequently, a child's grief may be slight when a grandparent dies. The child's only real concern may be for your wellbeing and wanting you to be happy again.

19. Death of a sibling. When a sibling dies, the surviving child has to face the fact, at an early age, that death is real and that it could happen to him or her as well. Often when there is an ill child in the family, the ill child gets much of the attention from parents, relatives, and friends. All the phone calls that come in are from concerned people asking about the ill child. Gifts appear, but only for the ill child. Trips are planned with the ill child in mind. You can understand, I'm sure, that this can create jealousy in the well child, even leading a sister, for example, to secretly wish for the sick sibling to die. When this happens and if the sibling dies, she will have to cope not only with the loss of her sister or brother, but with guilt, as well. She will feel ashamed for having harbored such thoughts, perhaps convincing herself that this wish was the actual cause of the sibling's death. Having reached this conclusion, she will be too miserable and ashamed to discuss the matter with her parents. In a case like this, a child needs to be told what actually caused the death and perhaps be made aware that other family members also sometimes harbored such thoughts during the frustrating weeks, months, or years during which they had to deal with the other child's illness (see Topics 61 and 62).

I remember vividly the meeting I had one day with the family of Colleen, a terminal cancer victim whose story I will relate in more detail later. (See the introduction of "Preparing for a Possible Death" at the beginning of Chapter 3.) The family consisted of the parents, eight-year-old Colleen and her fifteen-year-old sister Laura, who sat slumped and sullen across the room. After some discussion about what was happening in the family I commented that I felt pretty good about the way Colleen was handling the situation, but the person I was really concerned about—and I pointed to her—was Laura. Whereupon Laura bolted to her feet, pointed at me and said, "See, she is the only person who knows what I have been going through!" After some private counseling and help in setting some family guidelines on what should, and should not, be expected of this unhappy young lady, family life settled down and Laura began feeling better about herself and her dying sister.

20. The well child's need for reassurance. When a child is dying, parents are so caught up in their own grief and the extra work required that they often are absent, both physically and emotionally, from their remaining children. Under these circumstances a child may believe that once the death has occurred he will have his absent parents back and life will be normal again. But this seldom happens. The grief continues after the death, and surviving children often see their parents still unavailable to them and in great pain. At this point a boy may wish to have died in place of the brother or sister because the loss would not have been so hard on the parents. As a parent you should be alert to the possibility that your child feels this; it is not at all uncommon. Tell your son how much you need and love him and reassure him that you will be feeling better soon.

21. Death of a pet. When a pet dies, do not just place the dead cat or dog in the trash can or immediately replace the dead goldfish with a new one, hoping the child will not notice. A pet's death can be as painful for the child as the death of a person. Pets become part of the family and are included in family events. The death of a pet is often a child's first introduction to death, and this event should be treated as one would treat the death of a family member (see Topics 1 and 5). Talk to your child about death, decide what to do with the body, and discuss when to or perhaps not to get another pet. If you decide to get another pet, don't look for an exact replica, but rather look for a pet that is somewhat different from the one that died. Do not name the new pet by the old pet name; we don't want to teach our children that you can replace something that dies. But we do want to teach them that our hearts are big enough to love two or three different pets.

22. Children need to be prepared for whatever life has to offer. All life may be thought of as terminal. So how can you as a parent best prepare your child to accept this unpleasant reality and to cope with the painful losses he or she will face, sooner or later, such as the illness and death of a loved one? The next chapter provides suggestions on how to do this.

chapter 3

COPING WITH THE REALITY OF DEATH

The idea that all life must end—that everyone we love, everyone we care about, and each of us will die some day—is probably the most difficult truth we mortal beings have to deal with. A measure of our maturity is the degree to which we are able to face and accept this painful reality.

By definition children are not mature; they are just beginning to learn about life in its many aspects—its richness, diversity, and promise. That it will end one day is the aspect of life they are least prepared to grasp.

Thus when death approaches for a loved one—a parent, a grandparent, or a brother or sister—a child needs help in understanding what is happening. When death occurs, a child needs help in accepting the reality of the loss.

PREPARING FOR A POSSIBLE DEATH
▼ ▼

Eight-year-old Colleen (mentioned in Topic 19), with whom I worked some years ago when she was dying of cancer, taught me just how far a child can go in preparing for a death—be it her own or that of someone she loves. Not only did Colleen know that she was going to die, but the plans she made revealed her quiet acceptance of this reality. For example, she decided that since she would never be able to marry, she wanted to be buried in a wedding dress, and her parents took her in her wheelchair to choose a white lace dress to cover her body in the casket. One day she asked me, "When people die, don't they have a will? I don't have a will." She then told me that she wanted to prepare one giving her Barbie doll to a certain friend, jewelry to another, and so on, thus disposing of all her cherished possessions. It nearly broke my heart to listen to all this, yet I realized that she was dealing realistically with the painful reality facing her.

While I hope that your child never faces such an awful fate, Colleen's story may help you realize that young children can deal with sad truth, wrenching truth, even the most devastating truth—and handle it in their own way.

23. Don't hold back important information; let your child know when a loved one is seriously ill and faced with possible death. Often when a loved one is seriously ill children are not told, perhaps in the hope that illness will pass and there will have been no need for them to worry. This is a mistake. For one thing, all sorts of nonverbal signals will tell them that something is happening—worried looks, hushed conversations, telephone calls in the night, relatives showing up, perhaps less contact with you, and general household tension. For another, if death does ensue, they will have been left unprepared for the event.

A child kept uninformed about something so important to him or her is likely to draw conclusions that are wrong and that only create more anxiety for the child. For example, the child might think that a hospitalized father is staying away because he doesn't love the child anymore. Or the child might think that the illness of a loved one is contagious and that he or she might catch it, too. Children need correct information given to them in language they can understand. For example, you could say, "Daddy is in the hospital because he is sick with cancer. It's nobody's fault. It is different from having a cold or flu, and you can't catch it from him. You can still kiss him and hug him and tell him you love him." To make sure your child understands what you have said, ask him or her to repeat to you what you have said and invite your child to ask questions for further clarification. Ask your child if you have used any words he or she doesn't know the meaning of. Children need to know that they will not be kept in the dark when important things are happening. Knowing this saves them from endless anxiety.

24. In times of domestic upheaval, children continue to need boundary-setting and discipline. Boundaries are important to children because they are not ready to deal with all the choices, both good and bad, that the world has to offer. The corollary to boundaries is discipline, yet these controls often are put aside at times of shock, grief, and domestic upheaval. "Oh, let her go; her Mother is so sick," someone will say. Thus the child learns an important means of manipulation: "My Mom's sick so I should be able to have favors and get away with things." Don't let this happen. Household rules should remain in force as much as possible. With all the changes suddenly happening around him or her, a child could imagine the world falling apart. In order to feel secure and to know that life has not been totally disrupted, your child needs the usual rules and daily routines to continue as well as they can.

25. Visiting the seriously ill. When family members live far apart—grandparents in one place, aunts and uncles in another—children may not see close relatives regularly and thus may not see firsthand a natural part of life: the aging process. In such cases, visiting an infirm or seriously ill grandparent or other important relative can be very traumatic if it is not handled well.

To prepare for a visit under such circumstances requires letting your child know in advance what is happening, using the correct language. If the person has cancer, call it cancer. Be prepared for some very direct questions, such as, "Will she die?" I suggest that you answer these questions as honestly as you can but also that you leave room for some hope. You might say, "Yes, she could die, but the doctors are doing all they can to help her live." Then talk to your child about feelings, about being scared, mad, or sad, or about other feelings he or she may have. Ask your child how he or she is feeling right now. Then share with him or her how you felt when you first heard the news. Finally, ask what you could do to help your child feel better.

26. Does your child want to visit the ill person? Ask your son or daughter if he or she would like to go. If the answer is "no," then find out why. Most often it will be because your child is afraid of strange places or

unknown things. Usually, once the matter has been discussed, he will elect to go along. However, never force
him to visit if he absolutely does not want to go. At the
same time, be prepared to support him later if he begins
to feel guilty about not having gone. This happened with
my son, then ten, who was terribly uneasy about visiting
his dad in the hospital. He reminded me that his dad had
said he didn't want the children to see him as he was. I
think that the idea of a visit to his dad was very frightening
to him. I supported his reasoning at the time. Later, when
he began to feel guilty about not having gone, I reminded
him once again that I had supported his reasons for not
going and assured him I still believed he was right. He
seemed more relaxed after that and was able to put that
concern aside.

**27. Prepare your child for the visit by talking
about the setting the ill person is in.** What kind of
medical equipment is in the room? If you need information
about this, you might call the nursing station or the special
nurse taking care of that patient. What kind of noises are
there? What odors might be smelled? What does the room
look like? Is it a hospital room or is it a living room that
has now become a bedroom? Then talk about the physical
changes your daughter or son will see. Talk about the way
the ill person used to look and how that person looks now.
Then look for some diversions to ease your child's anxiety,
such as bringing a gift for the ill person. This might be a
picture she has drawn or a letter he has written, a cassette
tape he has made or one he could make there with the ill
person, flowers picked from the yard, a small gift the two

of you have selected and purchased, a game or puzzle. If it is a holiday, the two of you may want to bring something symbolic of that holiday.

28. Taking a gift to an ill person can be helpful.
It can serve as a diversion for your son or daughter. Visiting a seriously ill person can be a disconcerting and difficult thing to do. If your child has brought some sort of a gift it will give him something to do and will provide him with a natural subject to talk about. It also will give him time to take in the surroundings, relax, and feel that he has done something helpful. I remember my seven-year-old daughter's visit to the hospital to see her father, who was in a coma at the time. Since it was the Christmas season, we purchased a small artificial tree and took it home so she, her brother, and two sisters could help decorate it. The tree soon was covered with popcorn and cranberry strings. Glass balls and tinsel were added, and the tree looked great. The three older children didn't yet feel ready to go to the hospital but were able to send a part of themselves, since they all had a hand in preparing the tree. The tree gave my daughter something with which to occupy herself while sneaking peeks at her comatose father.

Another reason for taking a gift is that it provides a way to say goodbye. It is a common practice whenever someone moves away to provide the departing friend with gifts. Gifts mark important events such as birthdays, holidays, anniversaries, baptisms, and confirmations. We leave a piece of ourselves with the receiver of the gift. It is a token of love or friendship between the giver and the receiver, an unspoken vehicle of caring when words are difficult to say. It can perpetuate a sense of closeness in the face of the prospect of physical separation. The same purpose is served when your child takes a gift to a loved one who is about to die.

29. The time spent on the visit should be short. Ten to twenty minutes is long enough for a child of any age to endure on a first visit to an ailing loved one. Perhaps the next visit will be less emotional and the child will be comfortable staying longer, be less fidgety and feel less eager to leave. After the visit, set a time aside for debriefing. How was it for your daughter? How did she feel? What thoughts does she have about the next visit? Talking, writing, and drawing are all ways in which she can express her feelings about what she saw and heard.

30. Involving your child in the terminal illness of a loved one will enable her to begin her grief work early. Preparing her in advance and giving her a chance to visit, say, a dying grandmother, will help her to get on with her life more readily when the death occurs. You might tell your child, "Grandma is very sick, but the doctors are doing everything they can to help her get better. We hope she will, and I know you hope she will. But we also know there is a possibility that she will die." By informing her of the seriousness of her grandmother's illness—and by gently bringing up the possibility that Grandma might die—you provide her with the opportunity to begin her grief work before the death occurs. Also, if she visits her dying grandmother, she will have had a chance to say goodbye to her—a critical element in the healing process.

In my own family I observed this process at work as my father wrestled with the advanced stages of Parkinson's disease. Every day his grandchildren and great-grandchildren streamed in and out of his farmhouse, dropping in for dinner or supper, tagging along as their parents came to visit, seeing the ravages of his disease but calling out cheerily, "Hi, Grandpa," and "How are you today, Grandpa?" I saw the older children helping their grandfather, lifting him from bed to wheelchair, even helping him get dressed or undressed. The fact that they could adjust so well to these changes in their grandfather reveals again how children can deal with grim realities when they know what is happening.

WHEN DEATH STRIKES
▼ ▼ ▼ ▼ ▼ ▼ ▼ ▼ ▼ ▼ ▼ ▼ ▼ ▼ ▼ ▼ ▼ ▼ ▼ ▼

Some years ago I had a call from a mother with a terrible problem. She told me that months earlier she had called for help when her husband, having threatened suicide, seemed ready to carry out the threat. Her two small children were away at the time. A SWAT team had arrived, calling to her husband with bull horns and then descending upon the dwelling with tear gas, breaking into the roof, crashing through a ceiling and generally creating havoc as the neighbors watched in amazement. It all proved to no avail as the disturbed man, using a gun, completed the act of suicide. The house was left in a shambles.

The mother's problem was this: after many months the house had been repaired, the worst tear gas odors dispelled, and it was ready to be occupied again, but she had yet to tell her four-year-old son or six-year-old daughter what had happened. When they stayed with relatives while the house was repaired, she had told them that Daddy was on a trip. Now what was she to do?

I agreed to meet with this worried mother and her children. I told the mother it was necessary to tell her children everything that they would be hearing from playmates and that she would need to start being honest with them, giving them the basic facts and then encouraging them to ask any questions that came to mind, particularly after they started playing with the neighborhood children again. I also met with the children for a time, and I am happy to say that they were able to accept this devastating news, and, I believe, continue to trust their mother in spite of the falsity of the earlier story she had told them.

Admittedly, this was rather late to start being truthful with them. It would have been far better for her to have been truthful in the beginning. However, because she told them the truth *before* they heard from neighbors any contrary version of what had happened, she avoided the most damaging effects of her false story. But what would have happened if she had continued to pretend that this awful event had never occurred?

31. Because you love your child, it's tempting to protect him or her from a loved one's death. Parental instinct seems to say, "This is more than a child can handle, so I'll conceal my real feelings and make up some story about what really happened." Or maybe, "I want her life to go on normally without having to worry or feel bad, so I just won't tell her anything and hope she simply forgets she ever had a mother." The father of a two-year-old daughter once called me after his wife had died following a long illness. Since the little girl had been without her mother's presence for some time, he wondered if he could just marry again and present the new woman as his daughter's mother. I don't know what happened because I never heard from him again after I said, "It's not going to work."

Don't fool yourself into thinking that you are protecting your child by shutting her off from reality or by telling her things that are untrue; the price for that could be years of needless anguish. Just reflect for a moment on what it will mean to carry that guilty secret for the rest of your life, or on the effect that its discovery some time in the future could have on your relationship with your child.

32. Simplicity and honesty are your best tools. When your child asks you what has happened or what is going to happen, answer each question with simple, honest words. Answer only the direct question. Don't give more information than was asked for. Your child will take what you have said, process that information, work or play for a while, and come back when she has more questions or needs more information. She will ask questions as she is ready to deal with their answers. If you are honest and direct, your child will know that she can count on you to be available and trustworthy. This sense of security is vital during a time when a child is dealing with loss.

FUNERALS
▾ ▾ ▾ ▾ ▾ ▾ ▾ ▾ ▾ ▾

I often share this story with my audiences to introduce the subject of children and funerals. It tells us that even at a very young age children are capable of attending funerals without traumatic effect: When I asked a group if anyone knew what you do at funerals, a first-grader, a handsome little boy, raised his hand and said, "You pray a lot." I asked him if he could remember any of the prayers. "Yes," he said, whereupon he folded his hands, bowed his head and solemnly began, "I pledge allegiance to the flag of the United States of America."

33. Should children be taken to funerals? After the death of a loved one you may wonder whether you should take your child to the funeral and you may worry about the effect of such a sad event on your child's well-being. Why not just send him or her across the street to be with friends and watch TV or play video games?

Why are funerals important? Funerals are for the living. They give us the opportunity to connect with family and friends, to offer love and support to one another. Funerals are occasions when an otherwise repressive society allows us to express our sadness through tears and crying. Unless there are very special circumstances (see Topic 42), it is my strong feeling that your child should not be denied the support or the opportunity for mourning that a funeral can provide.

34. Talking with your child about the funeral. In talking with your child about the funeral, begin by explaining what will happen there. Then ask her if she wants to go to the funeral. Never force a child to attend the funeral if he or she adamantly refuses to go, but very few children will say that they don't want to go (see Topic 40). If your child does say no, spend some time talking with her. You might ask her if she knows why she doesn't want to go, or what the scariest thing would be for her, or what the worst thing is that could occur there. I find that children who say no are usually afraid of what's going to happen and readily change their minds when you explain the ritual of the funeral to them (see Topic 39).

I can't emphasize enough the importance of preparing your child for that first visit to the funeral home and for the funeral itself. (See "Funeral Homes and Cemetery Visits" under Topic 94.)

35. Funerals help us accept the reality of death. When a loved one dies, the immediate impact is so powerful, so shattering that we want to dismiss it as unreal. Funerals help reconnect us with reality. As we look at the dead body of our loved one, or the casket that contains it, we have to accept that the death has occurred and let go of the fantasy that this person shortly will walk in the front door, alive and smiling. The ceremonies of death, the viewing, the funeral, and other rituals such as the Shiva tradition of Judaism with its seven days of intensive mourning, make death more real to us. They allow us to proceed with the grieving process by breaking through our denial and taking us toward acceptance of reality.

36. Even more than adults, children need confirmation of the reality of death. When this is possible and consistent with your religion and culture, seeing the dead body of a father or mother, grandparent, or sibling can be very helpful to your child because a child's vivid imagination so easily can fantasize that this loved one is only on a trip and will soon return. Without confirmation of the reality of the loved one's death, your child could spend months or years searching and waiting for the return of the deceased. Worse yet, he could come to believe that the loved one has simply *elected* to go away because he has done something bad or because that person doesn't love him anymore, and further, that other family members are lying to him about this. Given free rein to such fantasy, how could your child ever trust adults again or feel good about himself?

37. What if the body isn't presentable? When a loved one has been killed in an auto accident or a fire, or has even been murdered, the body may be damaged to the extent that it cannot be made presentable. In this situation, viewing the body as a confirmation of death might be unwise, even for those whose traditions otherwise would encourage this.

What you can do is have a person whom your child trusts identify the body and then convey directly to her that she has seen the body and that, sad to say, it is indeed the body of the loved one. Your child is far more likely to believe what she is told when it is presented in this way than if no special effort is made to confirm the reality of the death. Also, if this approach is taken, she always can go back to that person and ask again and again if that was "really my daddy in the casket," thereby gaining needed reassurance that the death did occur. If your child presses for information about the condition of the body, the initial response might be to ask her what she thinks it might look like, providing some insight into her fantasies. Knowing this, you or the trusted person can describe the body to her in as simple a form as possible without going into great detail. For example, she could be told that her daddy's body has some bruises or that the burn has discolored his skin. If her questions aren't addressed, however, there is no telling what her imagination might construct—possibly a picture even worse than what you are keeping her from seeing.

In difficult circumstances like this, when you are unsure exactly what to do or say, don't hesitate to ask for whatever professional help is available in your area. Your pastor, rabbi, family doctor, community hot line, or local mental health center may be able to tell you whom to call.

38. Funerals are for saying goodbye. As we gaze at the body or casket, we have a last silent conversation with our loved one. We can say goodbye. We can tell the dead person all the things we wish we had said before: "I love you," or "I'm sorry," or "I will miss you," or any words that we may need to say to help with the grief. Saying these words in the presence of the body will have far more meaning than they would have later when said alone. If the casket is open, notes can be written and tucked into the pocket of the deceased's clothing, perhaps with a small photo of oneself. Children need to be asked if there is anything they would like to have buried with their loved one. You may have an idea of what would be nice, but more often your child will have some very significant idea of his own. I also like to suggest that the child pick some garden flowers to place in the casket with the body. The funeral director should be told that they should remain in the casket.

Because we tend to associate gift-giving with goodbyes, it can be comforting for a child to offer a small gift, a note, a picture of himself, a picture he has drawn, or a flower as a parting gesture of love and devotion. I remember the funeral some years ago of a mother of six children, each of whom selected an article representing the special relationship he or she had with their mother. During the church service each child carried his or her gift to a table near the casket, in effect saying a personal goodbye to the mother he or she would never see again. Your child might want to do something similar.

39. Preparing your child for the funeral. Once, when I was meeting with a group of children after a death in their neighborhood, I asked them if they knew what one wears to a funeral. One worldly-wise eight-year-old raised his hand and said, "I think you have to rent a tuxedo." Children need accurate information to prepare them for new experiences.

Take time out to talk to your child about the funeral and the rituals that are going to be included (see Topic 34). Go over them step by step. If the casket is to be closed, explain to him what a casket is and what it contains. Explain why it is closed, perhaps for reasons of religion or tradition, but emphasize that his loved one's body indeed will be present in that box. Tell him that the funeral is a special service just for the deceased and that it has been arranged for that person's friends and family members to say goodbye to him or her. On the other hand, if the casket is to be open, discuss what a dead body looks like. Explain that the dead person will *appear* to be sleeping and that you may even find yourself waiting for the chest to rise and fall as if breathing. Tell him that this is different from sleeping, that this is death. Explain how a dead body feels to touch and that it is all right to touch the body. Explain that when you touch a dead body, it feels very firm, almost like the wooden arm of a chair, and that it will feel cool, not warm as it once did. And tell him that it is okay to kiss the body if he wants to, but that he doesn't have to. Tell him what will be expected of him, such as what to wear and how to behave. If the deceased is a close family member, share your ideas on how to respond when family and friends come up and say, "I'm sorry." Let him know that he can respond with a simple "thank you." Talk to him about feelings. Say that it is okay to cry if he feels sad and that others may be crying too. Explain that we need to cry when we feel sad, that we have to let these feelings express themselves. You might even prepare him for the possibility that something will happen that makes him want to giggle, and that if this happens it is nothing to be ashamed of. In times of intense emotion like this all sorts of confused feelings bubble up, and giggles can be a release for them. Finally, let him know what emotions you will be experiencing and what he can do to help you to feel better. Thus if you, as a parent, begin to cry, this will not be frightening to your child, and he will know that what you need is a tissue, a glass of water, or a hug. It will help him to feel that he is helping you.

Funerals and wakes last a long time, and it is difficult for most children to be present without a break. Make arrangements with another member of the family or perhaps with a friend to be available to take your child out for awhile, perhaps for a walk around the building, for some fresh air, or for a private cry.

Tell your child that the car which will be taking the body to the cemetery is called a hearse, that the family will be following it in a limousine or the family car, that a procession of cars will be behind them, and that when there is such a procession people turn their headlights on to let other drivers know what is happening. Continue to share with him the burial rituals: Will the casket be lowered into the ground while you are there? Will people throw handfuls of dirt onto the coffin? The more he knows, the more prepared he will be for this event (see Topic 45).

If it is possible, take your child to the funeral home before the wake or funeral to become somewhat familiar with the setting. This will make it less scary later on, when people and events may seem overwhelming. The more children can anticipate what is going to occur, the more comfortable they will be.

40. The child who refuses to attend the funeral. The child who refuses to attend the funeral, even after you have explained to her what funerals are all about, will need special attention. Find out who she will want to stay with while you are at the funeral. Try to make this decision jointly with her to head off future feelings of guilt for not attending. Later on, if she begins to regret not having gone to the funeral, be prepared to support this decision. Remind her that you agreed with her earlier reasoning and still agree with it. Describing the funeral or perhaps making a trip to the cemetery may help her feel that she had played some part in the ritual (see Topic 89).

41. Taking pictures of the funeral. Picture taking at funerals is a custom I see returning. Either a family member or friend can photograph the funeral. Funeral directors may also be willing to do this. The pictures of the casket, the body, and the flowers can be of great use later, especially when one has a child who refused to attend the funeral. The child thus can experience the event at a later date when he or she is better able to cope with it, free of the anguish felt immediately after the death. These pictures may be painful to look at early in one's grief, but they soon can become precious.

42. **When not to take your child to the funeral.** I can think of few circumstances under which I would not take a child to the funeral, other than if the child refuses to go. One reason might be to avoid a frightening scene that could occur. Example: You know that your great aunt Martha, being highly emotional, will do something like throw herself into the coffin of the deceased. Children should not be exposed to this. In such circumstances, I would arrange with the funeral director to have a special time for my child to be with the deceased when Aunt Martha wasn't around. During the wake or funeral, the child could stay with loving friends. With older children, you can talk to them ahead of time about Aunt Martha's emotional personality and discuss some ways they might help her if she starts losing control. You know your family best and how they behave, and there are times when you have to be aware of special considerations.

A CHILDREN'S FUNERAL
▼ ▼

This is a dream of mine, a new idea which you could consider if there are enough children involved to make it worthwhile. I'd like to include in the ceremonies following the death of a parent or other very close relative a special funeral service for the deceased's children and all the young cousins and friends as well.

43. Why have a children's funeral? A funeral is a final parting, a farewell, the last loving thing we can do for a loved one. A sense of peace comes in planning this last event, as well as a sense of closing this part of one's life and the emergence of hope for a new life. Yet children are usually left out of this planning, even though they, too, have feelings they would like to express and have the same need to bring closure to the part of their lives represented by the deceased.

If your child ever had a funeral service for a beloved pet, you may have observed how involved he or she became in planning the service and how much satisfaction your child received from carrying out those plans. I know from working with children that they take a keen interest in such rituals; there are many occasions when a special funeral service for children would be not only an enriching and deeply satisfying experience for the children, but a source of comfort for the adults who helped them plan it.

What would go into a children's funeral service? This would be a service of short duration, perhaps a half-hour, preceding the main funeral, or it could be a memorial service without the casket present. The service could be held at the funeral home or church or synagogue. A pastor or rabbi could be present to lead a prayer and also to make this an "official" funeral. In addition to the clergyman or other person officiating perhaps someone could be there to answer the many questions that run through children's minds—questions such as, "What is dead?" "Why can't I go with him?" or "Where do people go after they die?" (see Topics 11 and 12). The children would be part of the planning for this event and perhaps for aspects of the main funeral as well. They might, for example, help decide what clothes the deceased would wear and choose something to be tucked into the casket with the body.

For this special funeral the children could select the songs to be sung or music to be played and the prayers to be shared. The funeral itself would be an informal time when they could ask questions, say anything they wanted, and if the casket is open, touch the body. They could share memories, sing songs, and recite poetry or prayers. They could light candles (with supervision), have a procession, or have pictures taken. Allowing them to use their creativity could make this special event a tremendously meaningful experience for them and for you.

44. Planning a children's funeral. If the idea of a special children's funeral seems right for your child or children, I suggest the following steps:

1. Talk with the children who might be involved, finding out whether they are interested in such a special service.

2. If the answer is yes, discuss your thoughts with the funeral director and/or your rabbi or pastor and set a time and location.

3. Together with the children, plan who will be invited and call the parents involved.

4. With the children, plan the ritual of the service. Your pastor or funeral director could help you with this, but the children must do most of the planning. This is *their* service. Let them help decide on the poetry, religious verses, music, and other details. They may want to bring flowers, letters to the deceased, or pictures they have drawn to be placed in the casket or on a table nearby.

5. Set aside half an hour before the service. Use this time to prepare the children for their special funeral. No child should be brought directly into the funeral without time for preparation. Without that preparation, it could become a scary experience instead of a special time to say goodbye to the deceased (see Topics 34 and 39). During this "briefing" session, a member of the clergy or other informed person should talk to the children about what death is, what a dead body looks and feels like, feelings the children may experience, details of how the room is set up, and what they will be doing when they go into their special funeral. Children, like adults, want to know what is expected of them, where they will be sitting, what will be happening, and the order in which things will be happening.

6. Carry out the actual service as planned.

7. Have a short reception in another room with light refreshments to allow the children to talk about the service and to share their reactions with their friends and relatives. To release tensions, you could provide paper and markers for them to write or draw their feelings about the funeral.

A friend of mine, Bev, arranged a children's funeral for her husband, Phil, the father of two three-year-old sons, who had died of cancer. Having read about my idea in *Parents* magazine, Bev decided that she would like to have such a service. At first the pastor and funeral director were startled by the request. The look on the funeral director's face, Bev told me later, was one of sheer terror.

Before the service began, the children were told that Phil had died, that his body was in a box called a casket, that he would look like he was sleeping but that this was very different from sleep, and that they would be able to climb up to the casket to look and touch his body if they wanted to. They were also introduced to Pastor Pete. One young child started laughing, and the children were told that if they felt like laughing at any point, this was all right.

During the service the children sat in a circle on the floor, and the pastor told them a story about cocoons and butterflies, relating it to the life of the soul. The children were encouraged to ask questions, and then each got up in turn to place a flower on the casket and to look at and touch the body. They concluded the service by singing "Jesus Loves Me."

The questions the children felt comfortable asking will give you an idea of how such a service might go for you. They asked:

"If his body is going to be in the cemetery and his soul in heaven, where will his head be?"

"Where is this heaven, anyway?"

"Can Phil see us from heaven?"

"Can he drive a car in heaven?"

"Can God make Daddy better and then send him back?"

"Does God go to the grocery store and then cook for Daddy?"

Bev didn't tell me how she answered these questions, but since nothing is known about life after death, the safe answer in most cases would be to say just that. Of course, in responding to questions about a loved one's return, children must not be left with the impression that death can be reversed.

Bev said that the three-year-olds did a lot of squirming and playing around, the four-year-olds did a lot of staring, the five-year-olds had a number of questions, and the six- and seven-year-olds asked many questions and also cried. But most of the crying was done by the children's parents, who were observing the service from the back of the room, terribly moved by what they saw.

Later, one of the children asked Bev, "Why did Pastor Pete tell the story of the butterfly?" When Bev explained the connection, the child responded, "Oh, I didn't think it had anything to do with Phil."

This is important to keep in mind: children aren't quick to grasp the meaning of abstractions. Once I told some children an elaborate story about the life and death of a leaf, which I hoped they would relate to the life and death of a person. When I was finished, I asked them what they were thinking about. They answered in unison, "Dead leaves!" In explaining abstract ideas to children you may have to try various approaches to put them across. Like a teacher or college professor, ask for feedback; if they miss the point, try a different approach.

When the service was over the pastor told Bev that it had turned out to be a wonderful experience, and Bev heard the praises of the other parents for weeks to come. Repeatedly parents told her that the service had opened up their children to the subject of death and enabled them to ask many questions they otherwise would not have dared ask. Bev herself saw it as a meaningful and satisfying experience which helped her, too, acknowledge and mourn her husband's death.

THE BURIAL
▼ ▼ ▼ ▼ ▼ ▼ ▼ ▼ ▼ ▼

45. How to explain burial of the dead to children. After the funeral, something must be done with the dead body. Your child may think that it would be nice to just keep it in the casket at home so you could check on it from time to time. Remind your child about what happens to dead birds and other animals when they are not buried; explain that decay can spread disease.

A friend of mine tells a story from her childhood. She and her sister had tried to raise a chicken as a pet. When, in spite of their best efforts, it died, they placed it in a box labeled "BEWARE: DEAD CHICKEN" and put it on the windowsill of their bedroom. When, several days later, their mother found the source of a strange odor, their chicken-raising days were over.

In talking to your child, explain that putting a body into a pretty satin-lined casket is not enough, that we still need to do something more to provide proper care for our loved one. So we close the casket and seal it and take it to a place where many bodies have been taken, a place called a cemetery (see Topic 49). There it will be placed in a grave which is dug out of the ground. It will be buried in a nice spot where we can go anytime we want to feel close to our loved one. We can visit there as often as we like.

46. How to explain cremation to childen. If you or the deceased person have elected cremation, this decision needs to be conveyed to your child along with an explanation of what cremation involves, pointing out that a dead body feels no pain. You should explain to your child that as practiced in this country, cremation is not burning the body in fire—a practice that might be difficult for the child to accept. Rather, the body is put through intense heat, so intense that the body becomes ash. This is done at a special place called a crematory. The ashes are placed in a wooden box or an elaborate urn. Children are curious and may want to open the box and look at the remains. If your child makes such a request, look at them yourself first so you can describe to your child what it will look like. Is it dusty-looking ash or are there bone fragments that can be seen? It is all right to share this with your child. Then let the child decide whether to proceed further.

Also, you may wish to decide with your child what to do with the urn or wooden box. Do you want to bury it at the cemetery in a regular grave or in a special place called a columbarium? Or do you want to take the ashes to a place that the deceased loved and scatter them there, returning nutrients to the soil and helping plants grow? This might be in the mountains or at the seashore or at some other spot meaningful to your family.

47. Plan a time for you and your child to be with the deceased before cremation. Usually when a person is cremated it is done quickly. If possible, arrange for a time when you and your child can be with the body for a short while before the cremation is carried out. This is a very special time, a time for you and your child to confirm together that the loved one has really died. And it is a time to talk to the deceased and a time to say goodbye.

◄ 97 ►

Don't let the time pressures you may be feeling deprive you of this special time with your child (see Topic 36).

48. What is a memorial service? Memorial services usually happen after a body has been cremated, generally a week to several weeks after the death. They are similar to funerals except that the body is not present. Often a photograph of the deceased is on view to help set the scene and to remind everyone of the person who died.

CEMETERY TRIPS
▼▼▼▼▼▼▼▼▼▼▼▼▼▼▼▼▼▼▼▼▼▼▼▼▼▼▼▼▼▼▼▼▼▼

Cemeteries are monuments to and reminders of our mortality. Little wonder, then, that they make us a little uncomfortable and unsure whether we want to visit a cemetery after someone we love has been buried there.

Can a visit to the cemetery be helpful in dealing with your child's grief? The case of fifteen-year-old Grace may help answer that question.

Grace's mother had had a sudden and violent death which had shaken Grace badly. Weeks later her grandmother brought her to me on the recommendation of a school counselor, who saw that Grace was having problems concentrating on her studies. Grace talked calmly with me, showing no emotion whatsoever, recounting what had happened as if it had happened to someone else.

How could I get Grace to release some of her feelings? I asked her if she had been back to the cemetery since her mother's funeral. Since she hadn't, I asked if she would be willing to have me take her there. She assented, and her grandmother also gave permission. The two of us made a trip to the cemetery. What happened then is worth telling.

At first we couldn't find the grave. I was looking in one area while Grace searched nearby. Suddenly I noticed that she had stopped, that her head was bowed, and that she was weeping. I went over to her and put my arm around her. "Is this it?" I asked. "Yes," she sobbed, "but my mother's grave doesn't even have a marker!" The sight of the still-unmarked grave and the feeling that she was near the body of her mother had broken the dam. At last her stoic defenses had broken down and she could release some of that pent-up emotion. I suggested that she find some sticks and make a temporary marker for the grave to serve until a permanent monument could be put in place. She readily responded to this suggestion. Tying the sticks together with weeds, she placed a cross on the grave with tears still streaming from her eyes. The symbolism was tremendous; she was doing something important for the mother who had been taken from her so abruptly, so cruelly, without a chance to say goodbye. In the weeks that followed I was able to help Grace work through much of the anger she was feeling and to get on with her life.

While Grace's experience is far from typical, it tells us that there are times when a visit to the cemetery can help a child express grief.

49. Handling cemetery visits. After the funeral, there is usually a procession to the cemetery. There the ceremony continues, after which family and friends usually go to the home of the bereaved family for food and more time to be together. As in Grace's case, the question arises afterwards: Should we take the children back to the cemetery? How can it help?

I believe you should give your child the opportunity to return to the gravesite at least once after the burial, just to see if it is helpful. Does your child find it comforting to be near the loved one? Or does it mean nothing? After all, the loved one isn't there anymore; it's just the mortal remains of what was once a living, breathing, thinking person.

Plan the trip to the gravesite in advance. The length of time you stay can be short; ten minutes may be enough. You or your child can take flowers and place them on the grave. Flowers gathered from your yard or from a nearby field are always nice. Graves also are good places to leave notes, perhaps dealing with some unfinished business you or your child may have with the deceased or relating what has been happening in school (see Topics 83 and 84). Occasionally cemeteries have places where families can have picnics. This is especially nice as it encourages families to stay longer and teaches children that cemeteries can be pleasant and not always connected with sadness.

My own family used to make frequent trips to visit graves of relatives when I was growing up. There was only one problem: I had been led to believe that something terrible would happen if you stepped on a grave. So every time we arrived there I would ask, "Which side of the tombstone is the grave on?" I lived in mortal terror of making a wrong step. Be sure your child doesn't entertain such superstitions.

After that first trip to the cemetery, find a place where

you and your child can debrief. This may be in the car on the way home or at a local fast-food place for a soda. Ask questions about the cemetery visit. Was it hard for her? What part was hard? What part was nice? What kinds of feelings did she have? Share your own feelings with her. Was it hard for you? Which part? Do you want to go back? What ideas does she have for the next visit? With all of this behind you—the wake, funeral, burial, sitting Shiva, and cemetery visits—you and your child are better prepared for getting on with your lives.

50. Some things to be alert for after a death. As events following a death unfold, your child may be exposed to unthinking comments by relatives and friends which only create new anxieties. For example: "God loved your dad so much that he took him to heaven to live with him." The child is left to believe that *he* didn't love his dad or mom enough, and therefore his parent was taken away (see Topic 12).

One comment made to a boy whose father had died was, "You're the man of the house now. You must take care of your mother and sisters." Having heard this from a relative he respected, this young boy went out looking for a job and made plans to move into his mother's bedroom in his attempt to assume the role of father/husband. (See "You Have to Take Care of Mom" in Chapter 7. Also see Topics 76–79.)

Since, in spite of your best efforts, a relative might make such statements to your child, it is important to be alert to inappropriate role playing or other responses as the first days and weeks pass.

The best way to avoid problems is never to force a

child to do something that he is adamant about not doing. I now see as clients adults who as children were forced to do certain things against their will, such as the girl who was held over the casket and told to "kiss Grandma good-bye." For some thirty years thereafter she could not bring herself to enter a funeral home or attend a funeral.

Open communication is very important in forestalling such trauma. Talk with your child. Explain what is happening and what is about to happen. Invite your child to talk to you about what he is thinking and to ask the questions he has on his mind. Then listen to what your child is saying to you. In so doing you can correct false impressions, avoid doing things that would create future problems, and develop a stronger bond with your son or daughter than you ever had before.

Through all this be aware that children have many different emotional responses to their bereavement—not just sorrow, but such reactions as anger and guilt—and that they need help in finding ways to express those feelings. The next chapter provides specific things you can do to help your child work through these powerful emotions.

chapter **4**

▼▼▼▼▼▼▼▼▼▼▼▼▼▼▼▼▼▼▼▼▼▼▼▼▼▼▼▼▼▼▼▼▼▼▼▼

DEALING WITH YOUR CHILD'S EMOTIONAL RESPONSES

As with adults, children follow different paths through their grief, having different reactions at different times. Even if you have several children, all dealing with the same death loss, each child's grief process will be different. In one family I know in which the father had died, the oldest daughter refused to show any emotion or to cry, revealing instead intense anger and stoicism; a second daughter, much more emotional and quick to cry, was willing to share some of her feelings but bottled up others, inclining toward depression; the son became very quiet and withdrawn, revealing little of what he was feeling or thinking but showing signs of guilt; and the youngest daughter was the most accepting, feeling that her daddy was safe in heaven and that the family could now go camping and engage in other activities long put on hold. This is a fairly typical pattern of diversity in grief reactions.

The most common feelings experienced by children reacting to a death are denial, anger, guilt, depression, and fear. They may also develop psychosomatic reactions. You are likely to observe one or more of these emotional responses in your child, but probably not all of them. Just because your daughter hasn't experienced a response such as guilt or denial, don't get the idea that it is lurking around the corner, waiting to manifest itself. Your daughter may never experience that particular feeling. Or she may experience all the listed feelings in a single day and then start all over again the next day. Just keep in mind that grief is different for everyone, and use this chapter as a guide to educate yourself on what feelings your child may experience and on how to help her express those feelings.

51. Children need help in articulating their feelings. Because much of life still awaits them, children are only starting to identify feelings and to learn what to do with them. For the most part, children deal with feelings through some kind of acting out, sometimes in a disruptive manner, yet there are simple ways that you can help your child identify and express feelings.

Look around your child's room, note the materials she is comfortable with, and then see if these can be used as tools in teaching her about feelings. These materials might include paper, crayons, markers, clay, paper bags, puppets, dolls, old magazines, scrapbooks, balloons, a diary, a tape-recorder, books, or music. The key is that she be familiar with them and comfortable in using them. With some suggestions from you she can turn these materials into drawings, writings, collages, sculptures, plays, scrapbooks, or tapes: all centered on her feelings about the death of a loved one, helping her to express those feelings and to cope appropriately with them. In the course of these exercises she will learn lessons that she will carry into adulthood and possibly pass on to her own children.

DENIAL OR BLOCKING
▼ ▼

52. Faced with more than they can handle, children often step out of the real world into one they find more acceptable. Children have fabulous control over their imaginations, using them in everyday play. They have the ability to read a book or watch a television program and seem to enter into it. Blocking out the unpleasant is thus a natural thing for them to try to do when a loved one has had a traumatic death. They can just pretend it hasn't happened (see Topic 8). Often, children will say to me, "Can't we just pretend he is on a trip?" I have found children that can focus on a particular object so well they can block out what is going on around them. For example, one eight-year-old girl I worked with couldn't remember much about her parent's funeral, but she could draw the casket in minute detail. While children have this ability to block out painful images, it is important that over time they be brought back to reality and not be allowed to delude themselves into believing things that are not true. The way to do this is by gently providing them factual information.

53. The finality of death is overwhelming. The phrase "never coming back" is impossible for young children to grasp. In the everyday world we replace things. When something gets broken, we fix it; when something gets worn out or lost, we buy a new one. Following this line of thinking, I remember seeing a four-year-old boy whose mother had died. He commented to me, "Can't Daddy just go to the store and buy a new Mommy?" After once again telling him we couldn't do that, that Mommy had died and when you die, you can never come back, I couldn't resist asking him, "But if that were possible, how much do you think a new Mommy would cost?" He responded thoughtfully, "Maybe a dollar."

54. Coping techniques for denial or blocking. It is normal for the bereaved to be in a state of shock for a period, during which it is difficult to believe that a loved one is really gone. You wait for that person to return: for the car to drive up the driveway, for the front door to open, and for that familiar voice to call out, "I'm home." The length of this phase varies from two to several weeks depending on the suddenness of death, the cause of death, involvement with the illness before the death, communication between parent and child, changes in routine, and other such factors. Thus it is difficult to know when the normal period of shock is leading into a less healthy period of denial. Following are some suggestions on ways to gauge this and on ways to help your child if you perceive that he or she is having this kind of problem.

Talk to your child. Talking is always the best tool to use when working with your child. Use the correct vocabulary; dead is dead, not "gone on a trip." Using the correct words confronts the reality of the death (see Topic 2). Be open and honest, and ask a lot of questions so you can listen to what your child has to say. (See Topic 32.) Talk frequently. It is also important to try to be as flexible as possible. Children are ready to talk at unusual times and at unusual places. Be ready to talk whenever your child is, and look for times or places that are comfortable and nonthreatening for both of you. Talking may come naturally while driving in the car, fixing the lawnmower, or bathing the dog, or perhaps in the kitchen over a glass of milk before bedtime.

It is important right from the beginning to talk about the death and what happened, where you were when it occurred, plans for funerals and burial, and plans for the future. The more verbalizing goes on, the more real this will become not only to you, but to your child as well (see Topics 35 and 36).

Let your family and friends know how you are working with your son and ask them to support you. You may receive a lot of advice of what to do or not to do from well-meaning people, but the final decision on how to work with your child is yours. Remember that you know him best (see Topic 50).

Try to get to the bottom of his denial. Ask questions. If you don't already know, ask him how he first learned of the death and what he did immediately following that shocking news; however, keep in mind that he may not tell you *exactly* how he got the word. I remember a small boy who was asked to draw a picture of how he found out about his father's death. He drew a picture of his mother with her arm around him as they sat on his bed. He titled the picture, "Mom telling me about Dad's death." As he was leaving he turned to me and said, "That's not really how I found out. I knew before Mom told me. I heard our maid on the telephone." I suspect he would have told the same story to his mother, if asked. When a child is unwilling to talk about the death, that is another matter.

In discussing it with your child, be gentle but firm in explaining what happened and why the departed cannot come back to life.

In the case of a violent death, rumors often get started and need to be checked with correct information. Invite your son to ask questions or to come to you if he is hearing such rumors or stories about the death; he needs to know that you will seek out and tell him the facts as well as you can (see Topics 14–16).

A nature walk. Taking your daughter for a walk in a park or woods not only will provide an opportunity to talk but can help you get across the reality of death. Look for things that are dead, such as dead leaves or trees, dead insects, or a dead bird. As you examine these once-living objects, relate them to the loved one who has died. Any of these things can help you explain death to your daughter. Pick up the dead object, if it is safe to do so, and examine it. Talk about what it was like when it was alive, and the difference between being alive and being dead (see Topics 5 and 11). Again, using the correct language will help your daughter with the reality of death (see Topic 2).

A follow-up visit to the funeral home or cemetery. Another visit to the funeral home or cemetery could help overcome your daughter's blocking out or denial, reinforcing what really has happened. Let her explore the funeral home and ask questions (see "Visiting the Funeral Home" under Topic 89). Similarly, a trip out to the cemetery can be comforting to her, as she will see that it is a quiet, peaceful place with flowers and birds. These visits can provide still another time for her to ask questions and to become more comfortable discussing these matters with you (see "Going to the Cemetery" under Topic 89).

Books. Reading a book to your child that deals constructively with the subject of death can help you find the right words to say on a difficult subject. It can help your child replace fantasy with reality. But do take care when selecting the book and make sure it will further teach what you want your child to know (see Topics 3 and 4). Sharing a book with your child provides a normal, comfortable time together and again, an opportunity to talk to each other (see the bibliography).

Share your feelings. Sharing your grief, your tears, and your sadness will teach your son that these feelings are appropriate and that it is perfectly all right to have them. Since these emotions always reflect an awareness rather than denial of reality, it is good for your son to see you showing how you truly feel. Conversely, imagine how easily he could be led into a denial of his loss if you stoically held back all display of emotion, making it appear that nothing too serious had happened. However, since seeing Mommy or Daddy cry can be disconcerting to a child, be sure to let him know why you are crying and what he can do to help, such as provide you with a hug. Reassure him that you will feel better after you have had your cry.

Play acting. Observing your child at play can provide insight into what he or she is worrying about or thinking. Children often play out life situations. Don't be alarmed if you see your son reenacting a murder or your daughter planning a funeral with her dolls (see Topic 16). This is their way of "talking" about what is happening. At the same time, if you observe your son playing out the return of his mother or father from the dead, you will know that more needs to be done to make him realize that, much as we wish the dead could return, they cannot. As with adults, the more you go over the details, the more real it becomes. And it has to become real before a child can begin to work through his or her grief.

Don't be alarmed if your daughter goes up to strangers and announces to everyone within earshot, "My Daddy died." Don't scold her; this is a child's way of trying to digest what has happened. If this makes those strangers uncomfortable, that is a small price to pay for your daughter's acceptance of reality. In the event this should happen, support her by saying, "Yes he did die, didn't he."

When to be concerned. I worry about the child who leaves the room every time the deceased's name is brought up. This is a child who is trying to avoid the pain of his grief by attempting to block out the memory of the deceased. Spend more time with him in private, talking and gently asking questions, such as: I notice you leave every time we talk about Daddy. Why do you go? Does it hurt too much to think of Daddy? Is that why you leave the room? I miss Daddy, too. What do you miss the most? Always give reassurances and love. One cannot say, "I love you" too often. Let him know you need him and that things are going to be all right. Seek professional guidance if this goes on for longer than you feel is natural for your child.

Occasionally a child will develop a fictitious "friend" who is a replacement for the deceased. There may be requests to have a place set at the dinner table for him or space made for her in the car. Too much direct questioning or ridicule may cause this fictitious friend to go underground; however, it is important to ask nonthreatening questions such as: "What is your friend's name?" or "Does your friend have a little girl (or boy) like you?" or "How long do you think you will have this friend?" Gently keep reminding your child how much we all miss Daddy, but that he is dead now. If your child continues with this "friend" for any length of time, it would be wise to get professional help, as you want to make sure your child doesn't start to rely on fantasy to cope with all the stress that life has to offer.

There can be many variations of such denial. I know of a three year old who was so shaken by the death of a grandfather that, whenever the pain became too great, she assumed the identity of a friend who had not suffered such a loss and began addressing her own mother by the name of the friend's mother. I actually saw her do this in my office one day when the mother began to cry and her little daughter sought to comfort her by addressing her with her friend's mother's name. If you find anything like this developing in your child, you should seek professional help promptly, as this mother did.

ANGER
▼ ▼ ▼ ▼ ▼ ▼ ▼

55. Grief in children often manifests itself in anger and disruptive behavior. This is because the emotions generated by their grief, like the emotions of the adults around them, are powerful and confusing. Unlike adults, however, children don't know how to deal with these emotions. They will not yet have learned to identify, separate, and articulate such feelings, nor can they understand what is going on, why they feel insecure, or why they are so uncomfortable with the emotional changes they see and feel in the adults around them. As a result they are likely to feel overwhelmed and to respond in the only way they know how: acting out in anger, striking out at the people closest to them—younger siblings, friends, teachers, or their parents. If you understand what is going on, you can help your child through these difficult times. It will help both of you if you recognize that the anger directed at you in these circumstances is usually an attempt to convey an important message to you: "Fix it, Mom; fix it, Dad—put things back the way they were." Oh, that you could! But, even though you can't fix it, understanding your child's message is terribly important. It may be that he or she is angry with the deceased parent for dying and, being unable to communicate those feelings to the deceased, directs them instead to the living.

56. Anger is a powerful emotion. Anger is powerful and isolating and can feed on itself, becoming even stronger. It is like a tornado, gathering strength and then striking with a force which is frightening, not only to those toward whom it is directed, but to the angry person as well. Knowing more about anger can help you work with an angry child. Knowledge can help you avoid reacting in anger yourself in ways that can merely upset the child and lessen your chances of getting to the bottom of his or her anger.

57. Preparation for the parent. Before you begin working with your child on the issue of anger, take a close look at your own anger history. Think about your parents and how they dealt with anger. Were they the kind of parents who never expressed anger in front of you? Or were they open with their anger, perhaps involving you in an unfair manner? What were you taught as a child about anger? Many of us were told it was bad to get angry and were sent to our rooms until we were no longer mad. Often the anger kept building up until you lost control and exploded into rage, breaking a favorite toy or slapping your sister. Perhaps you were then punished once more. So you may have learned that anger is bad and destructive. If that happened to you, how did you feel about it afterward? Can you think of better ways your anger could have been handled? Understanding your anger history can help you in dealing with your child's anger.

Anger creates energy which must be released somehow, preferably in a way that does no serious harm to anyone—either the perpetrator or others. If it is not released, it can lead either to depression—internalized anger—or to explosive acts like doors banged, furniture smashed, and words said that can't be forgiven. The person who thus has released his anger is left with feelings of shame and guilt, hardly helpful at a time of deep emotional stress.

You need to teach your child that anger is a healthy emotion that can be expressed in an acceptable manner. Then be prepared to suggest some specific ways of dealing with it.

58. Talk to your child about anger. Look for opportunities to discuss this subject *when anger is not actively manifesting itself.* Ask your daughter: How does anger feel?

How do you know when you are getting angry? Ask your son: Where do you begin to feel anger first in your body? Does your head hurt? Do you feel like crying? Do your knuckles turn white? Answering such questions can help your child recognize when this emotion is starting to take hold. The answers will vary from person to person.

You might say to your child: "Let's try to think of a time recently when you were angry. What was happening? Describe it to me." You may be surprised how willing your child is to talk about this. In so doing, she will be discovering how anger feels. She will begin to identify that feeling when it comes up again, as of course it will. Then talk with her about things she may have done that caused trouble when responding to that feeling of anger. For example, were there toys broken, angry words said that can't be retracted, or a classmate or sibling struck? Talk about more appropriate ways that she might have responded to that situation. At this point it might be helpful to share with her some of your own childhood experiences. This could lighten a heavy topic and let her know that you get angry, too.

When you have provided your daughter with some insight into identifying anger, and have discussed ways of coping that are unacceptable or have gotten one into trouble by feeding the tornado, underscore the point that anger is a feeling that is okay to have and that there are acceptable, healthy ways to express it.

59. Help your son identify the particular things that make him angry. I find it useful to get out a pencil and paper and begin listing everything the child can think of that generates anger. Is it because Dad has died and left you alone, making you different from your friends? Is it because Mommy is crying all the time and has no time for you? Is it because all kinds of strange people are in and out of your house and you have had to give your bedroom to visitors? Is it because there is too much confusion and you don't understand what is going on and no one talks to you? Are you mad at the doctors who should have made Daddy better? When you look at the particulars, some of the power of anger is reduced. Verbalizing what your child is angry about can help him to be more objective and gain more control over his anger.

You may be able to do something about certain of those listed items. Does he really have to give up his bedroom when visitors come for the funeral, or could other sleeping arrangements be made? If he does have to lend his bedroom to visitors, perhaps some other changes could be made that would make it less difficult—letting him camp out in the back yard for a few days or sleep in front of the fireplace. There may be items on that anger list that can't be changed, but your son will feel better just having someone listen to him and hear his side of the story.

60. Coping techniques for anger. Remember that anger creates energy. We need to look at different ways to release that energy safely. Sometimes we have to expend it before we can even look at the particular things that make us mad. Below are some techniques you can use to help your child express her anger.

Clay. Modeling clay is a wonderful medium to work with. Children love clay and readily accept it. I simply buy regular clay found in the five and dime. It comes in different colors and is reusable. Because it can be a bit messy and can stick to table tops, working on paper makes cleanup easier. As your daughter works the clay to soften it, energy will be flowing out and the anger lessening. You can then ask her to construct something that makes her angry. It's fine if you also want to construct something that makes you angry. Let her see you using the techniques you are teaching her. After the object is constructed, encourage her to share with you what she has built and why. In so doing she will be learning to articulate her anger. Then let her decide what to do with the object. I knew a girl whose friend had been murdered; she constructed out of clay a man holding a knife, standing over a child lying on the ground. After she spoke about what she had made and how angry she was, she proceeded to pound the structure with her fist until it was unrecognizable. She said she felt better. Similarly, your daughter may decide that what she wants to do is to smash her clay creation with her fist or, perhaps, throw it down on the floor, smashing it flat as a pancake. Or the decision could be to do nothing about it. Perhaps it was enough just to construct it and then discuss it with you.

Physical activity. Other ways for your child to release the energy that anger creates may be through running; bike riding (in a safe place without motorized traffic); cleaning his or her room; hitting a punching bag or a pillow stuffed and tied off for this purpose; screaming in a room that has been designated for that purpose; bowling; swimming; playing soccer, football, basketball, or tennis; horseback riding; or cleaning the horse stall—anything that requires the child to move around and put out energy. Teach your child to connect the feeling with the activity:

"I am feeling mad, so I'm going to run around the house five times."

Drawing. Drawing is another medium that children feel comfortable using, and it is an excellent tool for the expression of anger. It is always useful to have crayons, colored pencils, felt-tip markers, and paper available.

To get started, instruct your son to draw a picture of something that had happened that made him mad. Ask questions as he works. What are you drawing? Why are you using only red? Where did this happen? After the picture has been completed, ask questions about how he handled the situation in the picture and look carefully at his response to that situation. Compliment him on any good coping skills demonstrated, or help him explore the possibility that there could have been a better outcome if other strategies had been applied.

I remember two young girls whose father was dying of cancer who were having behavioral problems at home and at school. Their anger was out of control; they lashed out at everyone. As they sat sullenly in my office, I pulled out a large sheet of paper and suggested that they start writing down the names of all the people they could think of that made them mad. As they wrote names, they discussed what it was about these people that made them mad. It was good to see them share these feelings and to discover that they shared some sources of their anger. I noted that my name wasn't on the list, but it would have been okay if it had been. To demonstrate that grown-ups get angry too, I added to the list a few names of people with whom I was angry. After they had completed their list, I asked them what they wanted to do with it. They decided to tear it up, and they did. By this time the office looked as if it had been snowed in, with little bits of paper everywhere. I asked them to clean it up, which they did. When I asked them later how they felt, the seven year old answered, "lighter." Anger is indeed a heavy burden to carry around.

Tape recorders. Tape recorders are wonderful to use for discharging anger. You can say anything you want, play it back, hear yourself exploding with rage, and then erase it. They're safe.

When my first husband was dying from a malignant brain tumor which had affected his personality, his unpredictable moods were causing many disagreements between him and our ten-year-old son. I wanted our son to have respect for his father, and yet I knew that some of what was happening wasn't fair. I spent some time talking with our son, acknowledging the anger he must be feeling toward his father. I shared some things that I was angry about, too, including his unfairness to our son. Then I gave him a tape recorder to use when he got mad. Later on he shared a piece of one tape with me which went like this: "I'm so mad at Dad, I'm going to let my hair grow until it reaches the ground!" The recorder became a tool our son could use to express himself, discharge some of his anger, hear himself expressing that anger, erase it, and then go back and watch a football game with his father, who by this time had shifted into a more benign mood.

Writing. Writing is an excellent way to express one's angry feelings, and a journal can be a convenient vehicle for doing so. When you approach your child with this idea, you must also make clear that the diary will be confidential and that no one will read it without permission. This must be made clear to other members of the family as well.

Your child might even consider writing a letter, possibly in the journal, directed to a specific person. For example, if your daughter is angry at the family doctor for not saving the life of the person who died, she could compose a letter to the doctor expressing these thoughts. This is a letter that probably won't be mailed, but it would make her feel better by discharging anger that needs an outlet (see Topic 1).

Keeping a journal needn't be a burdensome project. Some will use it more than others, but there is no need for your daughter to write in it every day. It's just a tool to express feelings whenever they need to be expressed.

Writing can also take the form of poetry or song writing, and again many different feelings can be expressed.

Puppets. Puppets can be useful in discharging anger. Working with puppets gives the child an opportunity to say directly to the other person (in puppet form) exactly what is making him or her mad, providing a good release for the pressure the child is feeling.

When to be concerned. If your child does not appear to get any relief from his anger after trying some of the ways listed above you may have cause for concern. You should be concerned, too, if your daughter's rage is harming another person, a pet, or herself, if it is causing her to act out in school, or if the anger is causing so much distress that she can't regain control. If she is being destructive, observe what she is destroying—be it ripping up the belongings of the deceased or trashing her own room—and see that this doesn't get out of hand. Whenever you feel uncomfortable with the anger exhibited, it is fine to seek professional help.

GUILT OR REGRET
▼ ▼ ▼ ▼ ▼ ▼ ▼ ▼ ▼ ▼ ▼ ▼ ▼ ▼ ▼ ▼ ▼ ▼

61. Feelings of guilt or regret are common after a loved one has died. Let me clarify the distinction: I connect *guilt* with a deed that has been done for which you are sorry, such as an argument in which you may have said, "I hate you." I connect *regret* with something you wish you had done, such as saying "I love you" more often. However, regrets are usually lumped with guilt, making the guilt last much longer and making it more powerful than it deserves to be.

Guilt and regret can be so overwhelming that they become deep, dark secrets to be shared with no one. Children overwhelmed with guilt and regret will appear sullen and depressed, unusually good, or will insist on blaming someone else for the death (see Topic 19).

Children usually do not understand the meaning of the word *guilt,* so I approach it in this way: "Let's talk about something that has happened that you now wish you had done differently." Using this approach, you can begin to clarify for your child the difference between something for which he needs to be sorry and something which he merely regrets.

62. Coping techniques for guilt and regret. Following are some techniques you can use to help your child deal with feelings of guilt or regret.

Drawing. All you need for this is a big piece of paper and markers or crayons. Ask your daughter to draw a picture of something that happened that she now wishes she had done differently. A young girl whose mother had killed herself drew a picture of her mother asking her if she had lied about where she was after school. In this drawing the young girl drew a picture of herself saying, "Yes, I lied and I'm sorry." Making this drawing let her focus on something she had done that she felt badly about; further, it gave her an opportunity to apologize. Instead of this issue being suppressed, it was recalled, examined, and then put to rest. Giving your child a chance to draw what she is feeling bad about and to express what she wishes she had done instead can provide her with profound relief.

Puppets. Paper lunch bags make great, easy puppets. Give your child two bags, one for a drawing of himself and the other for a drawing of the person who died. Then encourage a dialogue between the two puppets. You can take over the talking for one if you want, or your son can put a puppet on each hand and carry on his own dialogue. This would be an opportunity for him to "talk" to the deceased and either apologize for something or talk about the regrets he is feeling. This technique will help him take care of unfinished business between himself and with the deceased: he may say such things as "I wish I had gotten a better report card before you died, but I'm going to do better next time," or "I wish I had told you 'I love you' one more time," or "I'm sorry I got mad at you" (see Topic 83).

Writing. Older children often prefer to work with

guilt or regret through writing rather than drawing. You can suggest that your child write a "letter" to the deceased. (Be careful when doing this with younger children: caution them that you can't really mail it. Many children believe you can write to Santa Claus and could very easily believe that they could actually mail a letter to Mom or Dad, Sister or Brother, in care of God.) Your child's letter can provide an opportunity to say "I'm sorry" or to express regrets of one kind or another. Or it can simply relate everyday experiences that the child regrets he or she no longer can share with the deceased. Some children may want to write in the form of poetry or songs. All of this is a fine way of expressing oneself and releasing feelings that otherwise might get buried, only to come out later in life.

Tape recorders. Tape recorders work well here also. Work with your child and help her to focus on something she wishes could be done over again and done differently. Voicing it to a recorder and hearing herself apologize will help ease the burden of guilt and regrets. Tape recorders are safe because they allow you to confess your darkest thoughts and then erase them. Do encourage your child to share some of these messages with you. When she can do this, she will be developing a relationship with you of trust and honesty, and she will be learning how to cope with one of the most destructive feelings one can have.

Games. Guilt is such a powerful feeling that it overwhelms other feelings. Guilt just makes you feel "bad." I like to play a simple guilt-relief game with children called "Remember the good things I did do." I might start with, "I'm glad I brought him his clean socks," and then ask the children to take turns recalling good things they did for the deceased. We often forget the good things that we have done when we are feeling guilty. Remembering these good deeds lessens the power of guilt.

Balloons. Balloons are priceless when looking for relief from guilt and other feelings. In my children's groups I encourage the children to write their secret messages on small strips of paper and roll them up into tight rolls so they can be inserted into balloons. The balloons are then blown up and tied off. Next we have a good time playing, "Don't let any balloon hit the floor." After a while, we stop and I hand out one pin. One by one the balloons are broken and the secret messages read by whoever happens to grab that balloon. It's safe because the children don't have to own up to their own secrets if they don't want to. However, they usually do. What a relief it is to them to find out that others have some of the same secret feelings they have!

You may want to use a variation of this approach for your child, perhaps not reading the message but tying it to a helium-filled balloon—or having your child write the message on the balloon—and then letting it drift off into the sky, carrying your child's guilty feelings with it.

When to be concerned. You may observe your child suddenly becoming "too good," doing everything he has been told, being terrified at making a mistake or not wanting to cause someone to get angry. He may experience anxiety about doing anything "wrong" for fear that would cause someone else to go away. If so, he is probably feeling in some way responsible for the death of the loved one. Or you may observe in your child a strong determination to blame someone else for the death. This could be an attempt to cover her own feelings of responsibility. Children feel very powerful in the roles they play in their families. Often they feel that if they had been present at the time of death, they somehow could have stopped it. I remember a girl, age fifteen, whose father had died from a heart attack. On the day he died, she had elected to leave for work five minutes earlier than usual, and she was convinced that if she had stayed home for those five minutes, she could have saved her father. We need to let our children know that they are not as powerful as that: that the death almost certainly would have occurred no matter what the child might have done to prevent it. If you are not able to help your child get some relief from these feelings of guilt or regret, don't hesitate to get professional help.

DEPRESSION
▼▼▼▼▼▼▼▼▼▼▼▼

63. A period of depression almost always follows a major loss. Watch your child's behavior. Are you observing any changes that make you uncomfortable? Does she seem to be tired all the time? Does she complain of not feeling well? School performance is a good guide; keep in touch with your child's teacher or counselor and find out what they are observing. I would suggest calling one of them once a week or more (see Topic 71).

The signs of a child's depression are similar to those of an adult—poor concentration (unable to follow favorite TV programs), withdrawal (spending more time in one's room and turning down invitations), not eating or eating too much, poor sleep habits, less interest in how one looks, constant sadness, crying more, hiding angry feelings, listening to melancholy music, and lessened interest in what is happening to others. Normally after a death a child's grades may drop for three or four weeks, but if there is no improvement after that, you have reason to suspect depression.

There will be a lot more talk about death after a loved one dies, and one can become preoccupied with it. The pain of grief can be so intense that one may also start wishing for death for oneself, as in a wish that one could just go to bed and not wake up or, when flying in an airplane, have it crash. These non-specific feelings are normal for adults as well as children. Don't be surprised to hear your child announce, "Today I want to die and go see Daddy." Young children believe this is a trip they can make and then return when they want. One little girl, on returning from vacation, told her mother, "Mommy, next year let's spend our vacation in heaven with Daddy." The finality of death just doesn't make sense to young children. If your child makes this kind of general comment, again explain the reality of death and reassure her of your love and how much you need her (see Topic 17).

64. Coping techniques for depression. There are many creative ways to help your child deal with "normal" depressions after a death. The focus should be on evoking memories of the loved one.

Drawing. Reminiscing is a healthy way to help your child through the depression of a loss. You might suggest to your daughter that she draw a favorite memory. Do one of your own, too. Then share them and just enjoy remembering. In early grief, memories may seem painful because they are a reminder of how much you have lost. However, with the passage of time they do a flip-flop and become treasures, like an old quilt that feels good to wrap around oneself. Memories are wonderful things; they are ours and no one can take them away from us. I also encourage the children to draw an unhappy memory. The reason for this is to keep the life of the deceased in perspective. One time, when a sixth-grader had died in an accident, his classmates were asked to draw pictures depicting their memories of him. When I noticed that all the pictures tended to idealize the dead child, I asked, "Didn't he ever do anything to bug you?" Soon I was seeing drawings of the boy spitting in their faces, throwing teddy bears up on the schoolhouse roof, and doing other not-so-nice things. The purpose was not to denigrate the child's reputation, but rather to help the children reconstruct a realistic memory of their classmate.

Too often, after death, the deceased is "sainted," and that isn't realistic. We all have our faults, and acknowledging this is not being disrespectful; it's just being honest. If your child's father has died and he is seen as perfect, how can that child ever love you with your many imperfections, or come to respect another man whom you may want to marry, or as an adult ever find a companion who could measure up to that perfect Dad, or ever love himself, since he feels so flawed by comparison with that "saint"?

Keepsakes. Keepsakes that the child has selected to remember a deceased loved one are often more valued than the ones which we, as parents, select for them. But all keepsakes have the potential to revive pleasant memories. Find opportunities to share these special items with each other. After my husband died, and after my children had selected their keepsakes, I selected more things to save that depicted his life and put these items in a trunk in my house. This trunk is filled with my husband's old Boy Scout uniforms, army clothes, pictures, and other memorabilia. Through the years as my children grew older, they became more interested in what kind of man their father was. What was their heritage? What kind of boy, husband, and father was he? Questions such as these prompt us to go upstairs and open the trunk and talk. This is such a good tool for conversation. You might want to do something similar to preserve memories of your loved one for you and your child.

Photographs. Looking at pictures is great for some and painful for others. Keep that in mind when suggesting that you get out that old box or album of pictures. Looking at pictures may be most useful for the child who is uncomfortable talking about the deceased. It is a safe, nonthreatening way to open communication. There will be tears as well as laughter. It helps make talking about the deceased part of the normal family conversation and thus provides something positive to counter the negative feelings of depression.

Scrapbooks. You might ask your son to help you put together a scrapbook about the person who died. Doing so is another way for your son to fight off depression, as it involves something he clearly wants to do: preserve the memory of the loved one. This scrapbook can include pictures, newspaper clippings, cards, and other items: a collection of things that will be a reminder of that person forever at your fingertips, a great record of that person's life to be shared later with other family members or grandchildren. I found it necessary to limit the number of scrapbooks a child should assemble after my experience with a young boy whose father had died. He happily worked on his scrapbook but became overwhelmed when his grandmother appeared one day with three grocery bags of things to add. Like everything else in life, a scrapbook project needs not only a beginning but an ending.

Videos or home movies. We now live in the age of video cameras, and these are wonderful tools to help with depression caused by death. However, some may prefer not to look at home movies or videos soon after the death, as it may be painful to see your loved one doing things that he or she will never do again. I find it is easier to look at still photographs and save the home movies and videos until later, when they will become priceless keep-sakes.

Games. Younger children respond readily to games. Try the game of "I remember when." Example: "I re-member when Daddy fell into the pool." Your child or children will pick up on this game quickly, eager to share their "I remember when" stories. Again, tears and laughter will ensue.

Plays. How about a play on the life of the deceased? Children love to act, and if you have more than one child, you might want to encourage them to make up a play about the person who has died. As you watch their pro-duction, you will gain much insight for follow-up con-versations with your child.

When to be concerned. Be concerned if you see depressive symptoms in your daughter not lifting two weeks after you first observe them. Keep in close touch with her teacher or school counselor and let him or her know your concerns. Perhaps the school could have an evaluation done on your daughter to keep an eye on her depression. This would allow you to enter her into therapy and work on the depression early.

Also be concerned if you find your child more peoccupied with death than you are comfortable with. For example, she may constantly talk about death, draw about death, listen to "death" music and perhaps even do dangerous things, such as hanging from a tree branch, carelessly stepping out in front of a car, or asking questions about how she could kill herself. If you observe any of this, seek professional help immediately.

FEARS
▼ ▼ ▼ ▼ ▼ ▼

65. The death of a loved one tends to shatter the child's perception that the world is safe and secure. When a parent or other important figure in their lives dies, children no longer see their world as safe and secure. They sense the upheaval as family members readjust their roles within the family structure (see Topics 76–77 and 79). They see and experience the explosion of emotions following the death. They see a surviving parent crying and emotionally unavailable to them for a while. Things happen around them that they don't understand. They hear bits and pieces of conversations and try to draw their own—often incorrect—conclusions. Their daily routines, so important to their sense of security, are interrupted, making them feel cast adrift (see Topics 24 and 70). The home may become like a hotel as family and friends descend upon them. Bedrooms, once a refuge, may now have to be shared (see Topic 59). Discipline is altered. With all of these things that children need to feel safe and secure now disrupted, it is to be expected that they will become fearful.

During the days of shock following a death, you may find your child clinging to you, afraid to let you out of her sight for fear that you will also leave. She may whimper or whine in an attempt to express this insecurity. She may even want to sleep with you at night, again afraid of losing contact with you (see Topic 78). There may be bad dreams, which will wake her up during the night. She may want you to close all closet doors and draw the curtains so the bogeyman won't get in. Things she used to do confidently may now become problems, such as going to the bathroom alone during the night, sleeping with the lights off, going to the playground, or being left with a baby-sitter.

You also may see your child's behavior regress in other ways. She may return to thumb sucking, wetting her pants or bed, using baby talk, or crawling instead of walking. These are all attempts to retreat to a time when she felt protected and safe. An eight-year-old girl with whom I worked drew herself shopping with her aunt for "baby clothes" for herself. During this time she was also sometimes crawling and using baby talk. After some discussion, I asked her directly why she did these things. She responded, "Babies don't die so young," revealing a strong desire to retreat to a safer time in her life.

66. Coping techniques for fear. All of these behaviors are normal reactions and shouldn't last for a long time. Meanwhile you can do several things to help your child through her fears, worries and concerns.

Talk to your child. Talking is of utmost importance in soothing fears. Keeping your daughter informed and up to date on what is happening, who is coming to the house, and what is expected of her will help put some of this anxiety to rest (see Topic 32). She should also be told that she can come to you or to another person you designate for information at any time. Encourage her to ask questions, for this is the only way you can know what she is thinking.

Try to plan some time during the day or week just for your child and you. This togetherness time needs to be observed consistently so your child can count on it. It should become a time that is rich with intimate conversation and closeness (see Topic 6). During the hectic days following the death of my first husband, it was difficult for me to find a regular time for each of my four children. To solve this problem I used errand times for these conversations. One child would go with me to help with the errand, which always included time for a soft drink before we returned home. The children would look forward to that time and took care of their own scheduling, swapping time whenever necessary. Depending on your situation, you may find the same approach helpful, or you may have the luxury of a more leisurely pace. However you organize it, you will find that regular conversation with your child is the best antidote to his or her fears.

Identify specific fears. The fears children experience are many. They worry about real concerns that adults, too, find frightening and upsetting, as well as others that may have little basis in fact. You can be of real help to your child by assisting him in identifying the specific fears and concerns with which he may be dealing. Realistic or not, each of his fears can be dealt with if you know what they are. You will hear some of the following: I am a lot like Dad; does this mean that I will die, too? Are you going to die? Will you go away and not come back? Will you be able to take care of me? Will we have enough money? Are you going to get married again? Am I going to have a stepfather (or mother or brothers or sisters)? Where will we live? Can we still go to Disney World? What if a bad guy comes in at night and kills us? What if a fire happens? What will happen to me if you die?

Once you have helped your child identify specific fears, you can address them one at a time to give him the reassurance he needs. For example, my children were worried about what would happen to them if I died. First I reassured them that I was healthy and that, as far as I knew, I would be around for a long time. But just in case I did die, who would they like to live with? They selected a favorite aunt, and she agreed. However, this aunt lived in another state, and my children still worried about how they would get there. So we went further with a "fire drill" and worked out a plan that they could follow upon my death. Knowing all this, they then could let this worry go and devote their energy to something else.

Drawing. There are times when it is difficult for a child to articulate his or her fears verbally, and drawing can provide an excellent alternative. If your child is having this difficulty, you could give her paper and markers and suggest writing at the top of the paper, "I worry about . . ." or "I am afraid of. . . ." Have her draw or write what is troubling her. As she draws, ask questions about her drawing and look for solutions that will bring her some relief from these concerns. The paper could also have the heading, "Before I go to sleep at night, I think about. . . ." Bedtime is the time when children are most likely to do their worrying, whereas they usually are capable of putting these things aside during the day when they are busy with other activities.

Dreams. Fears often emerge in the form of nightmares or dreams. Frequently, children will be unable to remember these dreams when they wake up in the morning but will experience some uneasiness before they go to bed the next night. They may anticipate that the dream will return. When your son cries out at night while having a dream, go to him, stroke him calmingly, and perhaps talk a bit about the dream. Some information on what is worrying him may come out in his dream life, and this could be an important clue for you. I also look for recurring dreams. These usually start the same way, then, before any closure can happen, the child wakes up, frightened and upset. Anxiety about going to sleep and dreaming the same bad dreams creates an unpleasant bedtime for the child. When I work with children on their dreams, I find that they can gain some relief by drawing the upsetting dream and then drawing an acceptable ending for it. This is a powerful tool, however, and must be used with care. Your child needs to feel comfortable in drawing his dream, secure in the knowledge that you will be there to reassure him if he becomes upset.

I worked with a six-year-old girl whose mother was dying from cancer. She experienced a recurring dream full of black snakes. After trusting me enough she drew her dream, filling a sheet of paper with black snakes. After she had drawn the dream, I asked her what she would like to do to those snakes and she said, "I think I would like to X them out." Which she did. She X'd them until you couldn't see any of them, and she continued to X them until the paper tore into shreds and she threw the drawing in the trash. She received immediate relief from this distressing dream and went on to tell her mother, who was having her own recurring dream about her house burning down, about this technique.

Another child, a boy aged seven, whose father had died by suicide, had a recurring dream in which his father came to the back yard to visit him. The nightmarish part was that his dad had no head. We spent time talking about the dream and then I asked this boy to draw it. He spent much time drawing the details, the grass, his father's shoes, and finally, the dream was completed. There was his dad standing in the back yard without a head. I made the comment that this was like a sad story that needed a better ending. The little boy picked up his marker and added the head. He has now gotten relief from this nightmare.

Balloons. Once you have helped your child identify her fears, you might want to talk about how she could let them go away in a symbolic way. Some time needs to be spent talking to her about the word *symbolic* and what symbolism means. Then you could buy a light-colored balloon, have it filled with helium, and let your daughter write her fears on it with a contrasting marker. Then the two of you can go outside so your daughter can release her balloon into the heavens, carrying her fears with it. (I once tried this by having children in my group attach notes to the balloon. Unfortunately, they were too heavy and the balloon wobbled off, requiring some quick thinking on my part to dispose of those fears and save the day. Luckily, I had a second balloon to increase the lift.)

Routines. When life becomes unpredictable and children become scared and unsure of themselves, it is important to keep as many daily routines going as possible, even during the days of turmoil following a death.

If your child wants to go to school, I would let him go; there may be security there with teacher and friends (see Topics 70 and 71). You should also let him know that if he needs to come home, someone will come to get him. The death of a loved one, however sad and traumatic, is a big event in your child's life. As with any big event, he will want to tell important friends. Going to school would help accomplish this purpose. However, once there, he may become restless and begin to worry about what is going on at home. Someone may need to pick him up.

If possible at the time of death when family members arrive, leave your child's room intact as a place of refuge. Routines such as getting up, eating, and bedtime should be kept as normal as possible.

Discipline should also continue during this time, when children may sense that the rules have changed. Be careful not to fall into a lax mode, justifying bad behavior on the grounds that the death has created special circumstances. In order to feel secure, children need to know what their boundaries and limits are and that you are there to enforce them. When they feel that their lives are out of control, they need to know that you will do the controlling. Be careful not to fall into the patterns illustrated by such comments as, "Oh, her dad just died so let's buy her that toy." This can teach your child to use the death to get her way. I know of a child who had a lemonade stand with a sign that said, "My mother died." She made $40 in one afternoon. I know of another mother who spent large amounts of money (which she couldn't afford) on gifts for her children in an effort to make up for the fact that they didn't have a father any longer (see Topic 24).

Touch therapy. Children can never get enough hugs and safe touching. These simple, normal actions, combined with talking to your child, may be your best tools in helping him or her feel more secure during this period of upheaval. I cannot say enough for the healing power of touch, and the love that is generated through touch. Touch can be one of the most powerful tools available to help a child learn to feel safe and begin to trust in life again.

When to be concerned. Fears and worries are a normal part of grief. But I would become concerned if these fears and worries reach a peak and then do not begin to subside or if your child fails to get relief from any of the solutions that you offer. I would also be concerned if these worries and fears are interfering with your child's getting on with her daily routines, such as eating, sleeping, or going to school. It would be a good idea to relay this information to your child's teacher so the teacher can observe your child in the school setting (see Topics 70 and 71).

I would be concerned, too, if I discovered that my child was using the death situation to gain some advantage for himself or to get out of some trouble that he had created, using the death as an excuse for some undesirable behavior.

Whenever you have concerns of this kind, it is perfectly proper to seek out the advice of a professional who can help your child over the rough spots and make the task of raising your child a little easier.

SOMATIC REACTIONS
▼ ▼

67. The death of a loved one is a high stressor, and stress can create all kinds of physical problems for us. Stress in children often comes out as a stomachache or as a general "I don't feel well," without any particular symptoms. This may carry on throughout the child's life, not only when there has been a death but at other times as well. We are all familiar with our child's complaint of having a stomachache when there is a test at school or some problem with a friend or teacher.

When the death has been caused by an illness or disease, the child often picks up on the symptoms of that illness and may say such things as, "My chest hurts," "I can't breathe properly," "It hurts to bend," "My leg hurts," or whatever other complaint the deceased may have had. Children can become preoccupied with the symptoms of a particular illness, and this preoccupation can carry over onto a death caused by something else, perhaps a car accident. You may see your child overly preoccupied with your health, your driving, or your other habits, certain that the same fate will befall you.

68. Coping techniques for somatic reactions. Clear information will put your child more at ease. The facts about the death will give some relief. If the disease is one that your daughter or son could inherit, it will help to reassure your child that you will keep taking her for regular checkups and that the doctor will be on the alert for the first sign of trouble. A physical examination by the pediatrician will also give her some ease as to her own health.

It is also a good idea to talk to her about what other feelings she may be experiencing. Often "stomachaches" are a coverup for something else that may be going on, even just a general feeling of being sad and lonely.

When to be concerned. If the symptoms do not disappear in a reasonable time and if a trip to the doctor does not bring any relief you may have cause for concern. Be concerned, too, about the child who may be over-identifying with the deceased. A boy whose father had died of a brain tumor, for example, began to point out similarities between his father and himself, such as the fact that they were the only males in the house, that he had blue eyes like his father's, that he liked the color blue, as did his father, and so on. Soon he was insisting on wearing many of his dad's shirts and sitting in his dad's chair. Then he developed headaches. Eventually it came out that he was worried that he would also get a brain tumor because he was so much like his dad. A trip to the doctor and the reassurance given there caused these symptoms to disappear.

69. Remember, grief takes a long time. Be aware that your child will continue to grieve the loss of the loved one even as he or she gets on with life. Therefore, over time, continue to watch for signs of emotional responses needing your attention and help.

chapter **5**

▼▼▼▼▼▼▼▼▼▼▼▼▼▼▼▼▼▼▼▼▼▼▼▼▼▼▼▼▼▼▼▼▼▼▼

ADJUSTING TO A NEW LIFE

Much as we would wish it otherwise, your child's life after the death of a loved one will be different from what it was before. In the days immediately after the death his or her life may seem to be changed permanently for the worse, and yet we know that this is not necessarily true. Life has many facets and takes many turns, and in time the child may find life filled with every bit as much luster as it had before. It is the period of adjustment from the old life to the new that represents the challenge you and your child must face together.

BACK TO SCHOOL AGAIN

70. Returning to school. Your son probably will want to return to school as soon as possible. After all, school is a big part of his life. It is in effect his extended family where there are friends with whom to share news as big as this is. In addition, returning to school reassures him that life goes on even though someone has died. We need those reassurances along the way, because when someone dies it can seem to the survivors as if the world has stopped. The routine of school helps the child regain the security that so often gets lost at the time of a death.

You'll need to spend some time preparing for your child's return to school. Discuss with him what he would like you to tell the teachers and what should be told to friends and classmates. I find that children have very clear ideas of what information they want shared, but I would discourage the idea of not telling the class anything. I would discourage my child having "secrets" such as this one. During this time of adjustment to a changed life, your child will need the support of classmates who know what has happened. Let him know that, for the first day or two, if he needs to leave early, someone will be available to pick him up. Be specific in stating "the first day or two" so that he doesn't begin to use the death as an excuse to leave early a week or two down the road (see Topic 24).

71. Have a talk with the teacher. Before your child returns to school, have a talk with her teacher. The experience of one girl whose mother had died illustrates the importance of doing so. When she returned to school she was startled by an abrupt announcement on the school's public address system about her mother's death. It would have been better, I believe, if the girl had been consulted first so the announcement would not have come as a surprise. Such "news" shouldn't just be announced, but should be given some kind of preface which would prepare the children for something that is out of the ordinary: an important, sad bit of news that needs to be relayed to them. It also is necessary to take into consideration the circumstances of the death and who has died. The message itself, whether given by the child's counselor in the classroom or, if absolutely necessary, over the public address system, should be short, perhaps followed by a moment of silence and quiet discussion.

In talking with the teacher I suggest that you begin by telling him or her what has happened and what you have been telling your daughter. Let the teacher know that you believe the structure of school will be helpful to her healing and that you expect the teacher to continue on as usual. Give the teacher some ideas on how the other children in the classroom might be supportive of her. Children are not born with the knowledge of how to be supportive of one another, especially in such unusual circumstances as a death situation. One of the biggest fears children have is that a loved one may die, and here is an instance in which it had actually happened to one of their number. They may feel so uncomfortable that they say things that are very hurtful. I remember a young boy whose mother had died who drew a picture of a classmate taunting him by saying, "Ha, ha, you don't have a mother!" I doubt that this classmate had any idea of the pain he was causing.

Before your daughter returns to school, it might be a good idea for your child's teacher to discuss what has happened with her classmates and how they can be of help when she returns. For example, they could be asked for ideas on what to do if Susie starts to cry. Children will have ideas of what would help them if they started to cry and can then see how this would be helpful to Susie. They might suggest giving her a hug, getting a tissue, or even crying along with her. Another point of discussion might be: What can we do if Susie makes all sorts of mistakes in her spelling? The children can discuss why they should be understanding if this happens and how they could be of help to her in her studies.

The teacher might also bring up the question of what to say to Susie when she comes back. The teacher might suggest comments such as: "I was sorry to hear about your grandpa dying." Or, "I felt sad for you when I heard that your sister had died." This might be all that is necessary to say. Older children might want to add, "If you want to talk about her death, I'll be here to listen." The children might want to make a "Welcome Back" poster or draw individual "Welcome Back" cards to be given to Susie when she returns. Such a gesture of love will be readily welcomed.

Let the teacher know that you will need his or her help, and would like to know whatever observations he or she has of your child in school. Plan to call the teacher regularly to see how your son or daughter is doing with school work and school behavior.

72. More structure needed for homework. As is true for adults who are grieving a recent death, children find concentration difficult at first. You may read a page in a book, yet on finishing it have no idea of what you have read. You may be so preoccupied with the death that it may be hard to focus on anything else. Your mind wanders and you find yourself daydreaming. Naturally, this presents problems in getting schoolwork completed. The grieving child needs a more structured schedule than was needed before to get back on track. You can help by setting times for homework and minimizing distractions during that time. In any case, don't be surprised if grades dip for several weeks.

73. Holiday observances. Schools traditionally celebrate holidays, yet holidays that once were anticipated with pleasure may now be dreaded. Special care needs to be given the bereaved child on these occasions, especially on Mother's Day and Father's Day if the child has lost a parent. You and/or the teacher should talk to your son to let him know that this could be difficult and to ask him if he has any ideas on how to make it better. I recently met with a group of children planning a Mother's Day party who offered to share their moms with the children who didn't have mothers—a very loving, caring gesture (see Topics 80–82).

74. Grief groups. Check with your school to see if it offers any bereavement groups for students. Some schools now offer such groups during the school day and, from all reports, they are quite successful. If your school doesn't offer anything of this kind, perhaps your child's teacher or counselor might be interested in starting one or suggesting something along these lines for the school system as a whole.* It's also possible that the school counselor might know of such a group in the community. It has long been a dream of mine to see children's bereavement groups in the schools, as well as in the community at large, and I'm glad that this is starting to happen. To my mind it can't happen soon enough, because children need help with their grief when the wounds are fresh: when the anger and

---

*My chapter in Prevention in Community Practice *(New York: Brookline Books, 1991)* will be helpful for teachers or counselors interested in organizing and leading a bereavement group.*

guilt dominate their thoughts, and before long-term patterns of denial and depression set in.

75. When to be concerned. You should be concerned if your son refuses to return to school; this could be a child who is afraid to leave your side for fear that you will disappear or die, too. This could also be a child who has found a way to use the death to his advantage by getting out of something he would rather not do (see Topic 24).

You also should be concerned if your daughter doesn't want anyone at school to know what has happened and insists that you not tell anyone. Her teacher and classmates need to be told something, if only to head off hurtful rumors that otherwise are certain to arise, and to save her from the burden of keeping such a big secret. If you run into obstinacy on this score, you should try to find out why your daughter is feeling this way. Chances are, she doesn't want to appear different from her friends and classmates. Or she may not be sure how they will react and may fear that she will cry in front of them and become embarrassed. If in talking to your child you can get her to express her reasons for feeling this way, you can then go about putting her fears to rest.

Once she returns to school, it's important to talk to your daughter from time to time about her school experience and to find out what her classmates are saying and how they are treating her. If you sense any problems, you should discuss them with your daughter's teacher.

Finally, I would be concerned if, in talking to your young child or to the teacher, you notice signs of regression such as thumb sucking or wetting that do not stop after a week or so. These regressions can be very embarrassing to your child, especially if the other children are laughing at her (see Topic 65).

Again, you know your child's behavior and habits better than anyone else. If ever you become concerned, it can be most helpful to consult with a professional, either to ease your worries or to get started with needed therapy.

ROLE CHANGES
▼ ▼ ▼ ▼ ▼ ▼ ▼ ▼ ▼ ▼ ▼ ▼ ▼ ▼

76. Roles change following a death in the family. When a father dies, the remaining spouse is no longer a wife. When a mother dies, the remaining spouse is no longer a husband. When a sister or brother dies, a surviving sibling may suddenly be an only child. What once was a whole family is no longer that.

Responsibilities change as family members have to take on new chores to fill the gap created by a death. All at once there may be no one to mow the grass, cook the meals, wash the clothes, fix small appliances, pay bills, or be a playmate to a surviving child. When such roles or jobs have to be shared it's not surprising to find resistance. It's not just that children don't like taking on extra work; it's also that each time they do some new task previously performed by the deceased, they are reminded of that person's death.

77. Role changes to watch out for. Watch out for the boy or girl who has decided to assume completely the role of the deceased. It is tempting and comforting to let this happen, but you will soon have a very angry child on your hands. He may feel obligated to take on the role and

◀ 151 ▶

may be encouraged in this direction by well-meaning friends and relatives. Such is the example of a boy who was told that he was the "man of the house now" and that he needed to take care of his sisters and mother. So at age twelve this young man proceeded to make the rounds of local merchants looking for a job (see Topic 50, and the section "You Have to Take Care of Mom," in chapter 7). I know of a mother whose husband had died, leaving her with several children. Her oldest son, then fifteen, became the self-appointed disciplinarian of the family. Initially it was a relief to the mother to have help with the younger children, but it was very much resented by and confusing to the younger children. At times their brother was their playmate; at other times he was their disciplinarian. It was confusing to the fifteen-year-old, also. There were times when he was in charge, and then there were times when Mom was in charge. He also resented this added responsibility and in time became angry and verbally abusive to his mother because he still needed some freedom to be a young teenager.

78. Sleeping arrangements. Then there is the matter of who sleeps where. After a spouse dies, the most lonely time for the surviving spouse is bedtime, when one is most likely to sense the physical absence of the deceased. It is not uncommon for children to move into the surviving parent's bedroom. After all, the child may be having bad dreams or may be afraid of the dark. If the parent is also experiencing bad dreams or terrible loneliness, it may seem natural to share the bedroom to comfort each other. My advice to you is: Better not.

Having a child sleep with you usually means that neither of you will get a good night's sleep because of different sleep habits, and you could be starting a habit that will be difficult to break later. Children need to sleep in their own beds. If your son wakes up at night, go to his room for a few minutes and then return to your own bed. If your daughter is afraid of the dark, help her to get over that fear, perhaps by keeping a night-light on; sleeping in your bed will only perpetuate it (see Topic 66).

It is important to keep old routines intact. Keep everything as normal as possible. I know of a widower whose thirteen-year-old daughter was sleeping with him. "But she's just a little girl," he said. A thirteen-year-old girl is far too old to be sleeping with her father.

79. Using your child as confidante. Be careful not to confide too many of your own worries to your child. Find other family members or friends to talk with who can advise and counsel you. Remember how old your child is, and try to allow her or him to be that age.

HOLIDAYS
▾ ▾ ▾ ▾ ▾ ▾ ▾ ▾ ▾ ▾

80. Planning for holidays. Holidays, once anticipated with pleasure, may for a while be dreaded. If we think we can just ignore them and that they will slip by unnoticed, we are fooling ourselves. You can't escape them: the stores are filled with reminders. Halloween is barely over when Thanksgiving items appear on the shelves, and mixed with these items are the first signs of Christmas. Schools also have holiday observances (see Topic 73). People one meets on the street greet you with cheery holiday greetings. Thus it is best to meet the matter of holidays head-on and, however painful, to plan for them. Often the anticipation is worse than the actual holiday.

81. The first year. I find that holidays are the most difficult during the first year after a death. In the second year they may be better and possibly even looked forward to. Holidays will have different meanings for each member of the family, with each person putting a different value on each holiday. Some will be eagerly anticipated and others dreaded. Good family discussions are important to discover how each family member feels about the coming holiday. For example, you may be dreading Christmas. On the other hand, your child may be looking forward to the gifts, the tree, and the visits, and may be fearful that Christmas won't happen, putting added pressure on you to carry on.

You may find it helpful to make some changes in your holiday rituals the first time around so that the absence of your loved one will be less noticeable. The next time you may want to go back to the old traditions and rituals, and they will feel fine. For example, I know of a widow who, after reaching a family consensus, took her three children to an island in the Caribbean to spend the first Christmas after her husband died. It was a very different type of Christmas celebration but one which, because it was so different from past Christmases, they were able to enjoy. The following year they returned to old rituals, and by that time they were comfortable doing so.

Two holidays that will be hard on children after a parent's death are Mother's Day and Father's Day (see

Topic 73). Be aware that these holidays are coming and discuss them with your child. Does he have any ideas of how to handle it? Does she have a substitute Mom or Dad she would like to acknowledge on that special day—perhaps a grandmother, grandfather, or special friend to whom she could send a card or with whom she could share a meal? Mother's Day or Father's Day are also good days to pick flowers and make a special trip out to the cemetery in honor of the deceased parent. Going out to dinner afterwards is fine, too.

Be on the lookout for other special, less commercial, occasions that might be important to your child, such as mother-daughter or father-son banquets. Again, talk it over with your son or daughter and decide on just what you can do to make this a very special occasion for the two of you.

82. Other anniversaries. In addition to holidays, be aware of anniversaries, especially your wedding anniversary if your spouse has died. Is your child aware of what day it is? Is there something you could do together to celebrate it? After all, the anniversary of your marriage will always be an important day. I know of one daughter who always makes sure that her mother has a flower at her bedside on the anniversary of her marriage, aided by a local florist who always finds that whatever money the girl brings is "just the right" amount to buy the flower. Let your child know that it is okay to acknowledge this day.

The birthday of the deceased is another anniversary to plan for the next year or two. Even though someone has died, it's still okay to observe that person's birthday.

Another anniversary that may bring a tidal wave of emotions is the first-year anniversary of the death. As this time approaches, you may find yourself and your children reliving the final days of the death in a painful replay or countdown of those final moments of that person's life. The emotions can be powerful and overwhelming. However, in talking with dozens of families, I am told that the anticipation is much worse than the day itself. A few even forgot what day it was and missed the anniversary entirely. Once again, find out how your child feels about this approaching day. Is she feeling the same anxiety that you are? You should make plans for this day, too. Would it be better for you to go to work and your daughter to go to school, or is this a day when you should take time out and head for the beach or mountains? If your child wants to go to school, it might be a good idea to let the teacher know what day it is; don't expect people at school to remember. Otherwise, this might be a day for some quiet reflecting and perhaps a trip to the cemetery.

UNFINISHED BUSINESS WITH THE DECEASED

▼▼▼▼▼▼▼▼▼▼▼▼▼▼▼▼▼▼▼▼▼▼▼▼▼▼▼▼▼▼▼▼▼▼

83. Loose ends. When someone dies there often are matters that have been left hanging, incomplete, or unresolved—unfinished business between a bereaved person and the person who died. As the date of death begins to recede, you may find that there are issues that come to light that have never been shared or resolved and that are beginning to bother you or your child, preventing you from getting on with your lives. Following are some typical examples: *I never told my dad I loved him. I never told my mom I was sorry I lied about not going to the mall. I have finished my model airplane and I want to show it to my dad, but I can't. The very last time I ever talked to my mom I got mad at her, and now I can't say I'm sorry.* And one of the most important issues one has to cope with may be: *I didn't have a chance to say goodbye.* These issues are very important to those children who are worried about them (see Topic 61).

84. Helping a child with unfinished business. There are ways you can help if you find that your daughter has unfinished business with the deceased. Look for clues when observing her at play or when talking to her. Does something seem to be bothering her? Does she seem preoccupied? Ask questions to see if you can gain some insight into her thoughts: "If you could talk to Grandma once more time, is there something you would like to say to her?" Is she obsessing about things, such as telling you over and over that she loves you? This could reflect a fear that you might die, too, or it could be an indication that she has a secret need to tell the deceased person of her love. If that person died suddenly, it could show a need to say goodbye.

Having identified your daughter's unfinished business, what can you do about it? Consider several ways to help her bring closure to this relationship.

Drawing. Use the comic strip idea. Put four or five blank squares on a piece of paper and instruct your child to fill in the square with drawings depicting herself talking to the deceased. She not only will enjoy doing this exercise, but it will help her bring some closure to unfinished business with the deceased (see "Drawing" under Topic 62).

Tape recorders. Tape recorders are useful tools in imaginary conversations with the deceased. Recorded messages could be made by various family members and shared with one another if everybody agrees to that (see "Tape Recorders" under Topic 62).

Empty chair technique. Set two chairs facing each other, one for your child to sit on and the other for the deceased. I find it helpful to place a photograph of the deceased on the chair, as this helps keep your child focused. Then discuss with her what she might want to say if there were one more chance to talk to the person who has died. This will give her an opportunity to voice all of her concerns as well as the happy things she wants to share, and to say a proper goodbye. Once that is done, she should feel some relief and be able to put that concern behind her.

Puppets. Using brown paper lunch bags for puppets, have your son draw himself on one and on the other draw the person who died. Have him put them on his hands and start a conversation. As in the empty chair technique, this provides an opportunity for that last conversation that never took place (see "Puppets" under Topic 62).

Letter writing. I find letter writing useful for completing unfinished business. This is a very powerful technique and you may see tears as your child signs her letter. There is a finality experienced in letter writing that brings home strongly the reality of the death. Also, children must be made to understand that we can't really send mail to the deceased and that this is only "pretend." Even so, this letter should be exactly like a real letter with a date and a salutation such as "Dear Dad" or "Dear Sis." The letter should be as long as necessary to say what your child has to say, perhaps two or three pages, and then it should be ended and signed. If the child is too young to write, the letter can be dictated. Once the letter is finished, you and your child can decide what to do with it—perhaps keep it in a special box. I remember a girl who wrote to her deceased dad, "If I could, I would make you that peanut butter sandwich you wanted." Letter writing also gives children an opportunity to voice questions they have about heaven, and they will often ask what it is like up there. Having asked these questions or said these things, they always feel better afterwards (see "Writing" under Topic 62).

GETTING ON WITH YOUR OWN LIFE
▼ ▼

85. Disposing of the loved one's belongings. There is no set time to sort out the belongings of the deceased, deciding which things to save and which to dispose of, but I suggest that this be done somewhere between the second and sixth month after the death. If you try to do this too soon—which could be an attempt to play down the importance of this person's life—you are likely to give away things you will wish you had kept. On the other hand, if you wait too long to do this, you may be building a shrine, refusing to acknowledge the death. Attending to this sad chore is a recognition on your part that your loved one is really gone and that you are making a conscious effort to get on with your life.

Before you take such a step, however, be sure you discuss it with your child. There are likely to be certain possessions of the loved one which your child would like to keep as personal treasures, reminders of the brother or grandfather or mother who once played such an important part in her life.

It is possible that your child will resist disposing of any of the deceased's possessions. If this happens, you should reassure her that there is no possibility that the loved one will return and need these things. You should also make clear that disposing of them doesn't mean that you don't still love that person and cherish his or her memory (see "Keepsakes" under Topic 64).

86. Dating and remarriage. I would hope that for all of you who have had a spouse die there will be a day when you can and will develop a close relationship with someone new. Before this happens, however, it would be well for you to prepare yourself for the reactions your dating may generate in your son or daughter.

Even though your son may have stated that he wants you to get married someday, once you start dating you may be hit with a flood of unpredicted feelings. Even though your daughter has given you her assurances that it would be all right for you to start dating, when that happens she may have second thoughts. The main issue is disloyalty to the deceased parent, especially if your child finds herself becoming fond of the person you have brought home to meet her. I know of one woman who, as she was about to go on her first date, discovered pictures of her deceased husband appearing out of nowhere, pictures that had been put away for some time. In talking to her son, she discovered he was worried that she would forget his dad. After reassuring him that she could never forget his dad, she told him that, even if she did fall in love with another man someday, she had the capacity to love many people at one time. She also reassured him that she would certainly let him know if she felt she was falling in love and thinking of remarriage.

It is important to let your children know when you are thinking about dating. The less they have to guess about what is going on, the easier it will be for them to accept you in your new role. I know of a young man whose wife died, leaving him with a six-year-old son. In a conversation one night, the father said to his son, "Maybe someday I will find a new wife." To his utter amazement, his son said, "Where will I stand?" Very upset with this question, the father felt a need to reassure his son that, no matter what, his son would always have a place with him. This little boy went on to say, "You don't understand. Where will I stand *at the wedding?*" There are many occasions when, talking to our children, we need to ask many questions to make sure we understand exactly what they are trying to say to us.

I also find children resistant to parental dating because it constitutes yet another change in their lives. Having just gotten used to having only one parent, they now have to get used to that parent dating. I know of a boy who said to his mother, "Who needs him? We're getting along fine by ourselves." You may find your child putting up barriers to make it difficult for you to get out. For example, "stomachaches" may develop at about the time you are to leave, making you feel guilty about leaving. If this happens, make certain that your child is not ill, have a reassuring talk with him, and alert the baby sitter to the situation.

Then there is the matter of sex. Children have a hard time understanding that an "old" person like you has a need for intimacy. One daughter I know of told her mother, "You've done that once already." This mother of four children humorously reminded her daughter, "No, I've done it four times." Children over the age of ten may have the hardest time with this idea, since their own bodies are developing and they are very self-conscious about this matter of sex. I hear many different comments from children: "When he's here I don't know what to do. Maybe I should leave home or something." "She's too old to be acting that way; it's embarrassing." Or "It's a different world out there now; she won't be able to handle it."

One mother who was having more than the usual problems with her fifteen-year-old daughter came up with an interesting evaluation of the situation. She realized that since both of them were dating, a sense of competition had developed. She perceived that tensions between her daughter and herself increased whenever she was going on more dates than her daughter! There was an added problem from time to time when her daughter developed crushes on men whom the mother was dating. Pressures eased once the mother realized this and could be more patient with her daughter.

In contrast, younger children may yearn for a family like every other family they know—a complete family. I often hear of a younger girl or boy wanting to sit on the lap of a date and asking that person to read aloud before bedtime and tuck him or her in at night, a routine sorely missed when a parent dies.

87. The child as chaperon. Once you start dating, you may notice a change in roles. Your child may appear to become the parent and take on a protective role. One mother who had started dating told me that her children often scold her for coming in too late at night. They ask questions about where they went and what they did. Sounds familiar, doesn't it? I told her that she should limit her responses to what she feels is appropriate. Another mother came home one night after a date to discover a sign strung across the entrance hall that read, "Wake me up when you get home." I also hear of children who appoint themselves as chaperons. When her dad and a date were chatting in the living room, one daughter refused to go to bed, insisting on staying up as long as Dad's date was in the house. Only after her father insisted did she finally leave for bed, and even then most reluctantly.

If you have teenage children, they may be concerned that you have been out of the dating world so long that you most certainly will be taken advantage of. I know of one mother who was dating a man who stood her up one night. She pleased her teenage daughter when she asked her for advice on how to handle this situation. The advice she received was that the next time "Joe" called, she should just ask, "Joe who?" and hang up!

Whenever you bring a man or woman home to meet your child, that person will be sized up as a potential stepparent. Chances are, your son or daughter will have decided in advance not to like that person. It is difficult for children to see a stranger in their home, sitting in their father's chair or working in their mother's kitchen. They need time to get used to this new arrangement, as well as a chance to verbalize their feelings. You should talk to your son during a private time and let him speak fully. Let him know you are willing to hear his views. Did he like the woman or not, and why? My children gave me advice on whether they felt a date was a "keeper" or someone who should be told to "buzz off." I let them understand that they were not making the final decision on whether I would date this person again but that it was okay to have an opinion. At the same time, your child should know that it is not okay to be rude to the people you bring home. They should show respect to any guest in your house.

I have found that humor helps whenever one can use it. I know of a family where the children devised a 1 to 10 rating scale on likability for the people their mother dated. A number of unsuspecting men went through this test until the children became more comfortable with the idea of their mother dating and the rating scale was forgotten.

88. Every family is unique. Perhaps some of the issues I have explored in these pages don't apply to your family. Every family is different from every other; every death has its own unique circumstances. Where in some examples I speak of a parent death, you may be trying to adjust to the death of a beloved aunt who lived with you and took care of your child while you worked. Still, the needs of your child to resolve her grief and to get on with her life are essentially the same needs that other children have when a loved one has died. Similarly, your need to get on with your life is not going to be much different from that of all other parents trying to rebuild their lives after a grievous loss.

What remain to be addressed are the concerns of those parents who are learning about these needs of their children long after the crisis of death has passed. If that is your situation, I have not only reassurance, but some concrete suggestions to make in the next chapter.

chapter **6**

▼ ▼

IT'S NEVER
TOO LATE

Some readers of this book may be concerned because they didn't realize at the time of a death that their children needed help in grieving their loss. If you are feeling such concern, I want to reassure you that there is still time to address those needs. In fact, as you will learn in Chapter 7, people have been helped with their grief as late as thirty or forty years after a death.

HELPING YOUR CHILD AFTER THE FACT
▼▼▼▼▼▼▼▼▼▼▼▼▼▼▼▼▼▼▼▼▼▼▼▼▼▼▼▼▼▼▼▼▼

89. It's never too late to get your child started with grief work. Never fear; all is not lost if you didn't give your child the kind of help I recommend at the time of a death, or if there was something you left undone.

Not long ago I worked with three children whose father had committed suicide. Their mother had gone to great lengths to show them love and affection, to involve them in the funeral, and to explain what had happened to their father when, together, they had found him slumped over the steering wheel of his car in the garage. The only thing she hadn't told them was that he had committed suicide. She had explained his death as an accident.

As the mother tried to restore a more-or-less normal life to her children, she found them irritable and prone to quarreling among themselves, leading to frequent family blowups. Finally, she asked me what to do. I suggested family therapy but also said that I thought that she needed to look at the fact that the word *suicide* had never been mentioned. This had remained a secret between her and her children, and I wondered if that unfinished business was causing some of the problems. After they started meeting with a psychologist, a family friend killed himself in exactly the same way as their father had, by carbon monoxide poisoning. The time was right, and their therapist asked me to sit in on a family session and talk about suicide. In that session I asked the children, "What's it called when somebody purposely kills himself?" The ten-year-old daughter instantly replied, "suicide," revealing an awareness of the subject and perhaps realizing that it was okay, at last, to use that word. In the ensuing discussion the mother was able to explain to her children that their father, too, had committed suicide. She also explained why she had told them that it was an accident: she had thought it would be easier for them if they didn't know the real cause of death.

The air cleared at last, life at home gradually returned to normal. The fighting stopped, and the mother and her children were able to get on with their grieving and with their lives.

If you are a parent whose spouse or close family member died some time ago and you are now questioning what you did or didn't do, or are wondering about phases of grieving that your child may have missed, you can do a number of things even now to help your child share in that experience.

Talking. As soon as possible, find some time in which you can talk to your child about the death and funeral. Your conversation might start this way: "Kelly, I remember how upset you were when Charlie died. It was a terrible time for both of us. I wonder if we could talk about it." Find out how much she knows about what happened and fill in the gaps for her. Talk about the funeral and the burial and invite her to ask any questions she might have (see Topics 39 and 45). It might even be appropriate to share with her the reasons why you made certain decisions concerning the extent of her involvement. Children have a great capacity for understanding and for forgiveness. Talk to her about feelings. How did she feel at the time of the death and at the time of the funeral? How does she feel now? What was the hardest time for her? How does she think these things should have been dealt with? Is she angry with you for keeping her in the dark? (See also Chapter 4, "Dealing with Your Child's Emotional Responses," on feelings.)

Visiting the funeral home. It might be helpful to make a trip to the funeral home and review for your child the service that was held there. This would be an opportunity for him to see this mysterious place, explore it, and ask questions. Call the funeral director and explain to him why you would like to bring your child there. I find most funeral directors very interested in helping, especially with children. Then explain to your child that you will be seeing the room where Grandma had her viewing and possibly where the service was held. Invite him to ask questions as you tour the home.

Going to the cemetery. Some time ago a widower brought his seven-year-old daughter, Polly, to see me after being advised by her teacher that she was depressed and crying a lot. What I discovered was that six months after his wife's death the stricken father still could not discuss the death with Polly. She desperately wanted to talk about her mother, but she had no one to talk to.

Looking for a way to open up conversation between them, I suggested that the father take Polly to the cemetery. He said that he couldn't do that by himself. I then suggested that I go there with them, and he finally agreed. At the cemetery we had to spend a long time looking for the yet-unmarked grave, but when we found it, I borrowed a couple of flowers from a nearby grave which Polly could put on her mother's grave. As she did so, both of them began to cry. He picked Polly up and hugged her, and he began to talk to her. Suddenly I found myself a spectator as pent-up emotions poured out; it was as though I weren't even there. Later we had hot chocolate in a doughnut shop, and the two of them couldn't stop talking. The dam had burst. Since then they have been back to the cemetery several times, and both the hot chocolate and the conversation have continued.

A trip to the cemetery can serve another purpose: helping a child feel that he is experiencing part of what happened, if he wasn't present at the time. However, some preparations for a first cemetery visit will be necessary.

You should describe to your child what the cemetery looks like and why we have cemeteries (see Topic 49). Plan what you will do once you get there. For example, you might hold a short "memorial" service that he could help plan (see Topic 48). You might also go out into your flower garden and pick a bouquet of flowers to place on the grave or carefully choose a flower at a florist's. Or you might suggest that he draw a picture or write a note to take to the cemetery to place on the grave. Or, as I have mentioned earlier, you could suggest that he write notes on helium balloons that could be released at the gravesite to soar to the heavens. Usually it is best to keep this first visit short, allowing time for de-briefing later, perhaps while stopping somewhere for a soft drink or dish of ice cream.

Pictures. Occasionally people have pictures taken of the funeral and burial. If you took pictures, this could be a time to share them with your child to give her a visual experience of that ritual. I now see video cameras in use at some funerals and burial services; if there is such a record, it could help your daughter feel that she was somehow a part of these events even if she wasn't there. However, because pictures carry so much emotional impact—especially if they show stricken mourners—you may find this more than you or she can handle. In that case, I would leave this for a later time, when you are both more comfortable with it (see Topic 41).

Drawing. You might suggest to your child that he draw a funeral. This will allow him to express an idea of what occurred during that event. You could help by giving some details or perhaps adding to the drawing (ask permission first). This exercise can enable your son to depict what he would have liked to contribute to the ceremony, had he been there, such as selecting a bouquet of flowers or a favorite garment or piece of jewelry that the deceased could have worn. This will help him feel as if he had been part of the proceedings.

Attend a funeral. There may be an opportunity for your child to attend a funeral of a more distant relative. At this time you could review with your child what went on during the earlier funeral and provide her an opportunity to ask the many questions that children have. If you do this, you should expect that some of the emotions your daughter may experience at this particular funeral will be for the earlier death. Be there for her with hugs and reassurances. (See the sections on funerals, burial, and cemetery trips in Chapter 3.)

90. Doing your best is all that you should expect of yourself. Our lives don't fit neatly into molds. Of course you want to do the best you can for your child, but don't feel that you have deprived him if you haven't done everything I suggest. The important thing is for you to be aware that your child is capable of grief and needs your help in resolving it. Beyond that, doing your best is all that can be expected of you.

As an adult you, too, may be carrying unresolved grief from your own childhood, and it is to the child in you that my last chapter is dedicated.

chapter **7**

▼▼▼▼▼▼▼▼▼▼▼▼▼▼▼▼▼▼▼▼▼▼▼▼▼▼▼▼▼▼▼

RESOLVING CHILDHOOD GRIEF AS AN ADULT

Like Peter Pan, there are untold numbers of adults in the world who, in some important way, have never grown up. They never had a chance to resolve the grief, the sadness, the sense of terrible loss which they suffered as children when someone very important to them was taken from them by death. They have remained in this time warp not because their loved ones died, but because the adults around them, perhaps consumed by their own grief, failed to see how shattered they were or how much they needed to express their grief.

In the course of my work I have interviewed many adults who once carried or still carry unresolved childhood grief. The stories I am about to tell are among the more dramatic ones I have come across. I have no way of knowing how common they are, for very little has been written on the subject. Common or not, they tell us what *can* happen when children are not allowed to resolve their grief. Fortunately, in each of these cases the child-turned-adult ultimately went on to live a full and constructive life, demonstrating that grief can be resolved, even belatedly. I have changed the names and other details to protect the anonymity of my subjects, whose unresolved grief kept them locked for so long in an unhappy perpetual childhood.

THIRTY YEARS OF COLD CHILLS
▼ ▼

Mary, a forty-nine-year-old woman, told me that for thirty years after her father died she suffered cold chills every night at 9 o'clock. They were more than chills; her whole body was so cold that others, touching her arm or face, would confirm that her body temperature indeed had dropped noticeably. So every night at 9 o'clock she would have to take a hot bath, which was the only thing she found that would restore her body temperature. Then she would be all right until the next night at the same time. What was the cause of this recurring phenomenon? It took time with a very perceptive therapist to find that answer. The chills were linked to the time of her father's death and the way in which she first was told of it. Once Mary understood the source of her chills, they ended. Yet for thirty years she had endured this disturbing abnormality because, as a ten-year-old child, she had never worked through or resolved the great loss she felt when the father she loved so much and with whom she so closely identified, was taken from her.

What went wrong here, and how could this anguish have been avoided? Here is the story as Mary told it to me. She had spent the night of her father's death with a cousin. The next morning she was told to "scoot on home," that she would not be going to school that day. Arriving home, she was met by two women who told her to go upstairs to see her mother. The house was very quiet. Finding her mother in the bathroom taking a hot bath, Mary sat down on the closed lid of the toilet. Mary's words: "She kind of washed one arm and said, 'Your father died,' and then she washed the other arm. She didn't look at me." There was no explanation or touching, no acknowledgment that this would be devastating news to the little girl, no attempt to console her.

Mary doesn't remember leaving the bathroom, but she remembers curling up downstairs in a large wing-back chair for such comfort as a chair could provide. She remembers no one talking to her or consoling her.

"For a long time," Mary told me, "I thought I killed him." She said that she and her younger brother had been taking a bath together a week before his death and didn't get out of the tub when her father had asked them to, necessitating his coming upstairs to make sure his request was followed. After his fatal stroke, she was sure that this extra exertion was what proved too much for him and that if only she had gotten out of the tub, he wouldn't have died. Assuming such responsibility is typical of children, but in her case no one could disabuse her of this notion because no one asked her how she felt or what she was thinking. The cold chills were but one result of the unresolved grief that Mary felt over the loss of her father and the abrupt end to some of her greatest childhood joys. Mary told me she also discovered she had an "internal clock," of which she was unaware, which prompted her to break into uncontrollable tears every April 10. Again, this phenomenon ended when she finally remembered in therapy that April 10 was the anniversary of her father's death. "I couldn't understand what was wrong with me," she told me. Even today, after clearing up several such mysteries, Mary still struggles with memory blocks.

Thanks to her discoveries in therapy, Mary has gone on to lead a productive life. She has had a successful career as a nurse, and she now has a good adult relationship with her mother. But Mary suffered through years of anguish which could have been avoided if she had been given an opportunity to work out the terrible loss she suffered with the sudden death of her father.

"GRANDMA, WHY ARE YOU SO COLD?"
▼ ▼

When June, now a grandmother herself, was eight years old, she was told to be quiet around her grandmother, not to bother her, and to go outside to play whenever she attempted to visit with the loving grandmother who had become almost a second mother to her. June couldn't understand this, as her grandmother had always been extremely close to the little girl, having taken care of her for much of her first eight years. Now she was punished when she tried to crawl into her grandmother's lap. What was going on?

One day she was taken into the spare room of her parents' house, only to find her grandmother lying in the bed there. She was told to kiss her grandmother goodbye. June wondered, "She's in bed! Where could she be going?"

June's grandmother reached out her arms to June, and

the child began climbing into the bed. Immediately she was told to get down, and someone tried to pull her away as she clung to her grandmother. "Where are you going?" she asked. As she was taken away, kicking and screaming, she heard her grandmother say, "June, June, it's okay." And then she said a few words in Polish—words that had a special meaning for the two of them. Yet no one told her the one thing she needed desperately to know—that the goodbye kiss was to be forever, that her beloved grandmother was dying.

"I was so afraid," June told me, "that I thought my heart was going to come out of my throat." That feeling was to continue for the next half century.

The next time June saw her grandmother she was in an entirely different kind of bed and it had been set in the front parlor. It was a casket, but June knew nothing about caskets. In this strange "bed" June saw her grandmother wearing a dress rather than a nightgown. June herself was all dressed up in her silk dress, white stockings, and black patent leather shoes. No explanations were offered for this strange appearance of her grandmother. There was a stool in front of the "bed," and June began jumping up and down on it, saying, "Grandma, Grandma, get up. It's time to get up. We're all dressed up. Come on, Grandma, get up."

Finally June's godmother offered her a feeble explanation. "Grandma's gone to live with Jesus, so we aren't going to see her anymore."

June's Catholic upbringing had left her with the impression that Jesus, in the form of sanctified bread and wine, lived in a box called the tabernacle on the altar of the church. "How could she live with Jesus?" June thought. "How will she fit into the tabernacle?"

Then someone told her she could kiss her grandmother. "I was amenable to that," she said, "My godmother said I could kiss her on the cheek. It was like kissing a stone. I didn't understand it. My hands went up, and I'm touching her all over. I'm touching her hands. All I could say was, 'She's cold, she's so cold.'"

Everyone was crying, and shortly someone said, "Take her away." June was taken away, screaming "Grandma, Grandma!"

June remembers someone saying, "I told you not to bring her. I told you not to bring her."

What happened next illustrates why children need to be told the difference between sleep and death. Unless they are told, they are likely to assume that a dead person is merely sleeping.

June recalls slipping out of the kitchen thinking that she would help make her grandmother warm. She found an afghan and, climbing up so she could sit on the edge of the casket, she tucked the afghan all around the body of her grandmother, all the way up to the chin, saying, "Grandma, I'm going to make you warm. Why are you so cold? Why aren't you waking up? I don't understand. Aren't you warm yet?" Eventually someone found her there and punished her for this loving gesture, done in total ignorance of the fact that her grandmother was dead. "I couldn't understand why they were being so mean," she told me.

Finally, June's grandfather told her the basic truth she

needed to know. He picked her up, cuddled her, and told her that her grandmother had died. This she could understand, because her dog, her cat, and her fish had died. Yet there were many unanswered questions that left June wrestling with the terrible loss she had suffered.

Thinking about June's story, it may seem as though she was less mature and more childlike than some eight-year-olds today. That merely meant that she needed more attention and more affection, more hugs and kisses, and a lot more information than she received both during this time of crisis and in the weeks, months, and even years of readjustment that followed.

"YOU HAVE TO TAKE CARE OF MOM"

▼ ▼

"You have to take care of Mom." Those were the last words that ten-year-old David heard from his father, an ailing bookkeeper who died of a heart attack thirty-five years ago. They were preceded by the phrase, "If anything ever happens to me." He died that night, and David's response, "Of course," took on a meaning that has plagued his life ever since.

According to David, his mother, always dependent, came to expect her son to carry out this deathbed promise. He assumed the role of the husband figure: the leader of the family. Since he and his mother continued to live with her parents, that didn't mean going to work, but it did mean an end to his carefree childhood. "I felt it was my responsibility to comfort her," he told me. "Therefore, I couldn't show any emotion. It was impossible for me to do that because if I cried, she would cry. I was the rock. That changed my life. I think I have been 'the rock' for the rest of my life."

As David was growing up, his mother would remind him that he was to do certain things because he had promised his father he would. He was haunted by his deathbed vow: "I always had a sense that Dad was looking down and watching me. I had to behave. Dad was keeping score."

The result is that David has reached the age of forty-five still seeing himself as "the rock," never showing emotion. And he is still totally involved in the life of his mother (who is now in a nursing home) responding to her every whim, often to the detriment of his own wife and children. It is normal for children to take care of their parents as they grow older, but David's role goes beyond that: he is carrying out his father's command.

As we know, rocks don't cry, express sympathy or dwell on losses; neither does David. "I was always taught that boys don't cry," he said. Even today his way of dealing with death is not to express sympathy but to "talk about something else."

"YOUR MOMMY DIED. MY DADDY READ IT IN THE PAPER"

▼ ▼

Thirty-five years ago Nancy learned of her mother's death in a rather unusual way—from a kindergarten classmate as she arrived at school.

"Why are you in school today?" he asked Nancy.

"What do you mean?" Nancy replied.

"Well, your mommy died," the five year old said.

"No, she didn't," Nancy replied. "She's in Mercy Hospital."

"No, she isn't, she's dead," the little boy insisted. "My daddy read it in the paper."

Nancy became so upset that she began hitting her friend. A teacher broke up the fight.

At her grandmother's house, where she had been staying, Nancy learned the awful truth: "No, she's never going to come home again," the grandmother said.

"Why didn't you tell me? Why didn't you tell me? Why didn't you tell me?" Nancy asked. There was no answer, no explanation.

"I don't recall anybody else, ever in my whole life, talking to me about it," Nancy told me. "It was unfair."

By the time she got the dreadful news, the funeral and burial were over, and Nancy had no opportunity either to confirm her mother's death or to express her grief. Her mother had simply disappeared from her life, and Nancy assumed it was her fault: that she had been bad and was being punished.

Even as a teenager, Nancy lived in dread that her grandparents would die and that no one would tell her. She once told an aunt and uncle, "I'm afraid that someday they will die and I'll find out about it by reading it in the paper."

In what Nancy told me next we get some insight into how adults can, unknowingly, leave their children in the dark and their emotional needs unmet.

Not until she was forty years old did Nancy have the courage to ask her father why he hadn't told her that her mother had died. "I cried," she told me, "and I said, 'I really needed you to tell me that she had died. I needed you to tell me that it wasn't my fault. I needed you to tell me that it would be all right and that you would take care of me and all those things.' "

Her father looked at her. "You mean I *never* told you?" he replied.

"No, you never told me," Nancy replied.

"I can't believe that," her father went on. "You mean I never picked you up and hugged you and said your mother had died?"

"No, you never did," she said.

Her father was stricken. "I'm sorry that I never did that," he told her. "I should have. You really deserved for me to tell you that."

"You know, Dad," Nancy continued, "I have suffered my whole life because you never told me. And it was only this last year that I realized it wasn't my fault. I thought I had been bad and that was why she died.

"It was wonderful talking with him," she told me, "because, you know, while nothing can ever change the fact that he didn't tell me and should have told me, in that conversation it was almost as if he had. He realized that it was something I needed. The part of me that is the little girl inside of this forty-year-old body got something that she needed that day. It was one of the priceless moments of my life. The two of us just sat there and wept."

HOW YOU CAN RESOLVE YOUR OWN CHILDHOOD GRIEF

▼ ▼

91. As an adult you may have longstanding grief from your own childhood to resolve. If you find yourself more troubled than you think is normal about deaths, funerals, or losses of various kinds, or if you have trouble forming intimate bonds because you fear abandonment, or if you have feelings of guilt or anger under circumstances that don't seem to warrant such feelings, perhaps you should examine carefully the death experiences you had as a child to see if there is a connection. If you have painful memories of death experiences you had at an early age, there are things you can do to help those experiences become less burdensome and more acceptable to you. Here are some suggestions:

Preparation. Spend some time thinking back on your childhood and reliving that very early or first death experience. This task may be somewhat frightening, especially if the death occurred many years ago and continues to be emotionally overwhelming to think about (see Topic 1). If so, you might consider finding a therapist who will be at your side as you review that death experience you had as a child. I stress that this person should be a therapist, rather than a friend, because the amount of emotion you may feel could be overwhelming for you or for a friend. Feelings that may have been suppressed for ten, twenty or thirty years can be surprisingly powerful. Not having had a chance to be expressed, they are waiting to be released.

As you think back to a personal tragedy that has remained unresolved for so long, don't be surprised if you feel yourself returning emotionally to the age you were when that death occurred. A therapist can help you from becoming frightened as these "little girl" or "little boy" feelings emerge. Once they are released, you should feel lighter, as if a huge burden had been lifted, and you will begin to gain new insights into what has made you feel and act in certain ways all these years.

Books. You can prepare yourself by reading one or more books which address childhood grief at the age you were when this experience occurred (see the bibliography). The reason I focus on your age at the time is that while your life may have moved on in other ways, some part of you may still be marking time at the age you were when that terrible loss, personal tragedy, or shattering experience occurred.

Tape recorders. As you begin this exercise you might want to use a tape recorder. The recalling of this experience can be so full of information and insights that you may not remember it all later on. You might also want to make copies of the tape to share with special friends or family members. Much of what comes out on the tape will be a history of your childhood and is likely to be treasured by your loved ones. Or your tape can be heard only by you. Do whatever you are comfortable doing.

92. Reliving an early death experience. Find a time and place where there will be no interruptions. Get comfortable in a chair, close your eyes, and let yourself go back in time to the age you were when the death occurred. Think about what your life was like at that time. What childhood memories do you have? Who were the people that made up your family? Can you remember happy as well as sad times?

Then begin thinking about the person who died. What was that person's relationship to you? How old were you? How old was that person? What memories do you have of that person? What was the cause of his death? How did you find out about the death? Were you told by caring adults or did you overhear a conversation and have to draw your own conclusions? Were you told about it by a classmate, as Nancy was? Were the adults around you consoling to you or were they of a more stoic nature, hiding their feelings? What were your family's religious beliefs? What memories do you have of the visitation, funeral, or burial? The activities around those three events can often be most traumatic, as in June's story. As you explore these events, try to remember what feelings you had and how you were treated (see Chapter 4). Are there blank spots in your memory? If so, find a family member who can help you out. Was there a particular part of it that is still terribly painful today, such as what June experienced when she was told that she could kiss her grandmother? In her case there was no preparation for what it would feel like to do this, so when she kissed her grandmother's cheek, she discovered that it was as if she were kissing a stone. This left her badly shaken, frightened, and confused. Did you have a similar experience?

Think about your life in the period after the funeral and burial. Were the adults so grief-stricken that they could not bring themselves to talk to you, console you or even take care of your basic needs? Were you in a situation, such as David's, in which you became the caregiver to your parents or to other adults around you (see Topics 76–79)?

Now think about what parts of that early death experience have influenced your life as an adult. What feelings do you have today that seem to relate to that early experience? Connecting the past with the present may occur in bits and pieces over a long period of time, but each time you are able to put something together, you will feel better. You will be gaining more insight into why you act and feel the way you do. You will begin to understand yourself better and you will feel lighter as you put old, bothersome experiences away.

93. Look for opportunities to heal past wounds. It might be helpful to in a sense relive the troublesome experience you had and make it "come out right" this time. June, for example, now an adult and a grandmother, took her young granddaughter Jenny to see June's godmother, who was dying. By this time June had reviewed her early death experience and had come to realize what her needs were and what mistakes had been made by the adults in her life. Because she wanted things to be different for Jenny, she was able to help her through the death and funeral of her godmother in the way she wished her grandmother's death had been played out so many years before. Not only was Jenny saved the anguish June long endured, but June was left with feelings of fulfillment and contentment that she had not had before. These feelings were similar to the emotions Nancy felt when she finally confronted her father about his failure to address her needs at the age of five.

94. Other techniques that can help resolve long-term grief. Depending on your talents and abilities, you might consider several other techniques that could help you come to grips with your unresolved grief. Following are a few suggestions. You may think of others (see Chapter 6).

Drawing. If art is a medium you're comfortable with, make a drawing or a butcher-paper mural of a funeral or of the particular event that has been so burdensome to you. Draw it the way you wish it had happened. Remember what was missing at that time and add all the missing pieces. Find someone to share this with.

Writing. Even if you don't think of yourself as a great writer, this can be another excellent tool to use. Do it in journal form or write it in the form of a story. Think about all the troubled spots in that event and think about how you were wishing people would react to you. Make it right this time. You're in charge of this experience.

Clay. Think back to the funeral or the event that has troubled you all these years and re-create it in a way that's acceptable to you. You might construct a figure representing your mother holding you and another representing your father stroking your hair. Do whatever your fantasies want. Learn from this experience and share what you have learned with your loved ones.

Funeral home and cemetery visits. Perhaps the difficult part for you took place at the funeral home or at the burial site. If so, this is the place you may need to confront. (See discussion of funerals, burial, and cemetery visits in Chapter 3.)

I remember a woman who felt that funerals were barbaric and refused to attend them. She could not bring herself to attend a funeral where the body was on display. Memorial services, on the other hand, presented no problem for her. She related a story to me about her grandfather's death and funeral when she was about eight. No one had prepared her for the funeral event, nor had anyone explained to her what a dead body looked or felt like. She had walked into the funeral home totally unprepared, and the effect of seeing her beloved grandfather's pale, cold, hard body in the casket was more than she could bear. In fact, she told me that forever afterward she could not think of her grandfather without seeing his dead body lying in that casket. Still, she didn't seem to realize that this was why she couldn't attend funerals. Having made that belated connection, she can now begin working on reversing the effects of that shattering experience.

In visiting the funeral home or cemetery, you may want a trusted friend to go with you for love and support. Also, you may find you can't go through with it the first time you approach the funeral home or cemetery, and that's okay. You may find that your emotions are too strong for you to handle comfortably at first. Maybe the first visit should consist only of walking up to the building or to the gate and then leaving. A second visit might involve going inside and collecting some literature about funerals. The third visit could consist of talking to one of the officials for a few minutes and then leaving, and the fourth visit could be a tour of the building or locating a particular gravesite. You're in control: plan your schedule to meet your own needs. The next step might be attending a funeral or burial of someone—preferably someone who was not a close friend or relative, so you would feel less emotionally involved. After each of these trips you should plan time to discuss your experience and how you felt with a trusted friend, family member, or therapist.

One last healing consideration. If, through one or more of these techniques, you gain an understanding of how a painful early death experience has affected your life, perhaps you will have an opportunity, as June did, to make sure that your children or grandchildren are spared the years of anguish that you experienced. When a death occurs you can ensure that your loved ones' emotions and questions are dealt with differently and that they have someone they can talk to, someone who will explain things to them and who will console them. When you help them in this way you will be helping yourself as well, vicariously reliving your own experience, and making it come out the way you wish it had.

95. Unlike Peter Pan, your child within can grow up. While Peter Pan remained a child forever, real people want to grow up and to live normal lives. They want to be free of childish fantasies and the burdens of anger, guilt, or depression that can keep them, in some sense, in perpetual childhood. My experience tells me that neither you nor your child need fear such a fate if you accept that grieving is a legitimate and necessary part of life's process.

During times of family crisis, children need love, affection, honesty, and recognition of the great losses they are suffering. Children have minds. They have imaginations. If they are told the truth in a loving and caring way, and if they are allowed to express their grief, they are capable of accepting even the most painful and devastating losses that life has to offer.

Out of the devastation of a forest fire new growth soon appears, and the cycle of nature resumes. Out of the agony and desolation of a loved one's death you and your child can also find new life and hope. My message to you is simply this: be kind to yourself and to your child, be patient, and watch for those first green shoots to appear.

BIBLIOGRAPHY

▼▼▼▼▼▼▼▼▼▼▼▼▼▼▼▼▼▼▼▼▼▼▼▼▼

For Pre-School-Age Children

Doris, Sanford. *It Must Hurt a Lot*. Portland, Oregon: Multnomah Press, 1986.

> *A book about the feelings experienced by a child when a pet dies.*

Prestine, Joan Singleton. *Someone Special Died*. Los Angeles: Price/Stern/Sloan, 1987.

> *The focus here is on the feelings of a young child after someone special dies. It also gives the reader a concrete idea of how to help cope with those feelings.*

Stein, Sara Bonnett. *About Dying*. New York: Walker and Company, 1974.

> *A picture book for parents and children to read together. A striking photograph of a dead bird makes death very real. This is a book for very young children. It includes guidelines for parents.*

For Young School-Age Children

Fassler, Joan. *My Grandpa Died Today*. New York: Human Sciences Press, 1971.

> *A book about the love shared by a young boy and his grandfather. When Grandpa died, David cried along with the adults around him. In spite of his sadness David went on playing and eventually learned why Grandpa had not been afraid to die.*

Grollman, Earl A. *Talking About Death: A Dialogue Between Parent and Child*. Boston: Beacon Press, 1970.

> *Newly revised, this book is an excellent guide for the parent in talking about death to a child. The first part can be read by the child; the second part is a guide for the parent which includes recommended resources.*

Hughes, Phyllis Rash. *Dying is Different*. Mahomet, Ill.: Mech Mentor Educational, 1978.

> *This book helps children to see death as part of life. It invites questions and seeks to increase the child's awareness of life and death in its most common forms. A sensitive and honest introduction to a serious subject.*

O'Toole, Donna. *Aarvy Aardvark Finds Hope*. Burnsville, N.C.: Celo Press, 1988.

> *Aarvy Aardvark comes to terms with the loss of his mother and brother with the help of his friend Ralphy Rabbit. A wonderful story of loss and grief. This story needs a parent to translate the animal story into human terms and then to the child's particular situation.*

Slater, Dr. Robert C. *Tell Me, Papa*. Council Bluffs, Ia: Centering Corporation, 1978.

> *Children have many questions about death. This book takes the great unknown of death and through the words of Papa,*

an older man, "tells it as it is." The feelings that are triggered by death are explained and shared in a loving and caring context. The child will learn that feelings are normal. Feelings hurt, but feelings shared are feelings diminished.

For Older School–Age Children
LeShan, Eda. *Learning to Say Good-by When a Parent Dies.* New York: Avon, 1978.

Written for the whole family, this book opens the way to genuine communication between youngsters and adults. In simple, direct language, the author discusses the questions, fears, fantasies, and stages of mourning that human beings go through after a death.

Rofes, Eric E. and the unit at Fayerweather Street School. *The Kids' Book about Death and Dying.* Boston: Little, Brown & Co., 1985.

Fourteen children offer facts and advice to give young readers a better understanding of death.

For Children of All Ages
Krementz, Jill. *How It Feels When a Parent Dies.* New York: Alfred A. Knopf, 1981.

This is a book of personal stories from children aged seven through sixteen who describe their feelings when a parent died.

White, E.B. *Charlotte's Web.* New York: Harper, 1952.

This children's classic is the story of a spider who befriends a little girl and her runt pig by writing messages in her web. When the spider eventually dies, there is sadness combined with an understanding that death is part of life's cycle.

INDEX

▼ ▼ ▼ ▼ ▼

◄ 199 ►